A FAMILY GUIDE TO CONSTITUTION CITY

We the People

A Special Publication Produced by The Philadelphia Inquirer

Written by Ruth Apprich Jacob
Illustrated by Helen Driggs
Editor Jonathan Storm
Associate Editor Lisa Tracy
Copy Editor Paula Fuchsberg
Art Director Charles Chamberlin
Design Director Joe Curcio
Circulation Director Stanley Budner
Circulation Consultant Stan Binder
Publisher Norman Goldfind

Published By
THE MIDDLE ATLANTIC PRESS
848 Church Street, P.O. Box 945
Wilmington, Delaware 19899

ISBN 0-912608-41-2
Printed in the United States of America

The Middle Atlantic Press, Inc.
848 Church Street, P.O. Box 945
Wilmington, Delaware 19899

Contents

DATELINE 1787

SOME TIPS ABOUT THIS GUIDE

A NOTE TO YOUNG PEOPLE

This section is meant for you. But we hope you share it with your parents and teachers and other older people you know, just as you share your best toys. You're always nice when a grownup asks to goof around with your Lazer Tag, aren't you?

This guide can help you pick which Philadelphia places you'd really like to see. It can also help you stay away from the ones you think might be boring.

You'll probably need to take a grownup with you to most of the places we describe. If you bring this guide along too, it will make your favorite places more fun. It can also give you something to do if the grownup drags you to one of the boring places.

But you don't have to go anywhere to enjoy this guide. You can just stay home and read and play with it.

We admit that this guide is supposed to be educational. You'll learn some things about Philadelphia, about the old days, about some of the great men who helped invent our country and about the United States Constitution.

Mostly, though, we hope you have some fun. And if you get bored, just turn the page when nobody's looking.

A NOTE TO GROWNUPS

Should we credit P.T. Barnum for the phrase "children of all ages"? It was probably some circusman who thought it up, since it has the tone of circus hucksterism and since circuses, perhaps above all other things, appeal to children of all ages.

This special section is not exactly a circus, but it, too, is aimed at children of all ages. Throughout the year, there will be a deluge of publications — some splashy, most of them solemn — to honor the 200th birthday of the Constitution.

The Inquirer plans both kinds, but we thought it best to begin with something that is fun, not cotton-candy fun like a circus or parade, but something a little bit more nutritious.

As the Constitution brought the states together, we hope this section helps bring whole families together to play and learn.

We guarantee that all the members of the family — unless there's a professor of American history in the group — will increase their understanding of what the Founding Fathers did 200 years ago and of how, why and where they did it.

And we're pretty sure that children of all ages will have some fun as well.

— Jonathan Storm

THINGS TO THINK ABOUT

1. What are some of the freedoms we wouldn't have without the Bill of Rights? Why weren't they included at the very beginning when the Constitution was proposed?

2. What minority group and what majority group have especially profited from constitutional amendments?

3. Can you think of a state that was formed from another state without its consent? Why was that possible?

4. Taxes are unpopular with almost everybody. What if an amendment were proposed to remove the section of the Constitution that allows them?

5. Military service is sometimes unpopular, too. What would the United States be like without the provision for an army and a navy?

(Answers: Page 75)

PONDER THIS

(You'll find "Ponder This" throughout this section. Sometimes, there will be answers right below the questions — you should cover them with your hand if you want to ponder a while. Sometimes, when the questions ask for opinions, there will be no answers given.)

In the early 1800s, Washington, D.C., replaced Philadelphia as the capital of the United States, and the capital of the country was no longer also the capital of a state. Why do you think the early leaders of the country were anxious to put their capital outside of all state boundaries?

Who are the two senators from your state and the representative from your district? How can you find out how much they're paid?

☛Answers: Remember, the states were still pretty jealous of their independence and of each other's power. The leaders didn't want any one state to have the prestige and power of the national capital.

A reference book, such as an almanac, may list the salaries for senators and congressmen. Or, you can find by writing them in Washington.

The city and the county, like the state, were both quick to volunteer their buildings to the national government. This was certainly a bit of an inconvenience. Do you think different levels of government would be so quick to cooperate with each other today? Why or why not?

Today we have problems with air and water pollution, traffic control and crime. Which of these problems troubled cities 200 years ago? Who or what caused the problems then? Who or what causes them now?

PATHWAY TO THE CONSTITUTION

What if you were a delegate to the Convention of 1787? Follow the "Pathway to the Constitution" by being at the right place at the right time and then making the choices that will create the U.S. Constitution. Each decision leads you closer to the final document. The path is not a straight line. There were a lot of detours before the Constitution became reality.

1. May 1, 1787: First you have to be in a state that is going to send delegates. You live in:

a. Ohio
b. Rhode Island
c. Vermont
d. Massachusetts

(To find the right state, go to Page 47.)

DATELINE 1787

Delegates' job: To decide on destiny

The year is 1787. The place is Philadelphia. Several dozen men, among them some heroes of the American Revolution, have gathered and are meeting every day — in secret.

They meet in peace and freedom. England was defeated four years ago. The people of the United States of America are free of English taxes, free of the king, free to go their own way at last. It should be a happy time.

But it's a desperate time. The nation is in danger. These men — there will be 55 of them in all — fear for their country's very survival.

What's the problem? The United States is free — perhaps too free. The 13 states have agreed to a "league of friendship." But a league is not exactly a government.

It's true there's a Congress, but it has no real power. It can't force the states to supply any money. Without money, the United States can't pay an army to face the British who are still hanging around on the western borders, or to protect settlers against the Indians.

The country can't pay its debts either — debts that grew during the fight for independence, debts that are fast approaching $100 million.

There's a lot of quarreling between the states, too. Sometimes they actually fight battles over their borders. More often they compete for trade, and that makes everybody's money problems worse.

Pirates on the high seas are capturing American sailors and holding them for ransom. There's no money to rescue them.

It looks as if the country is just going to fall apart if something isn't done.

So a few leaders of the various states come back to the city where some of them signed the Declaration of Independence more than 10 years ago. Philadelphia is the biggest city in the New World, and a real center of business, education, culture and religious tolerance.

In 1787, it's also the capital of Pennsylvania, and its State House (which will someday be called Independence Hall) once again plays host to patriots, as it did during the Revolution.

Among these delegates are the best brains and the most politically experienced men of their time — and some not-so-outstanding fellows. But generally, they're an impressive group, and in public they appear calm and confident.

Privately, though, they confess to each other that they "tremble" for the future of their country. And they agree to meet behind closed doors and windows in the heat of summer. They agree not to talk to anybody until they can do the job they came to do.

They aren't even sure what that job is, at first. But by the middle of the long, hot summer, they know.

They have come to create a strong central government to hold the country together. The idea is revolutionary for its time. It's likely that if the citizens knew more details of what was going on, such a government could never be created.

The delegates fight over the job for four long months, and in the end they produce — four pages. Sixteen of the men have either walked out of the meetings in a huff or been called home on family business. But 39 sign their names to what is written on those pages.

It starts out, "We, the People of the United States, in order to form a more perfect Union . . . ."

It is the Constitution of the United States of America.

How did the delegates get to Philadelphia?

It was more easy for some than others.

George Washington rode into town in style on Sunday, May 13, the day before the convention was supposed to begin. He arrived in his own carriage from Virginia, with a military honor guard escort after he crossed the Schuylkill. Cannons boomed, bells rang, and thousands of people turned out to see the most famous man in America.

Ben Franklin didn't have to arrive. He lived here. He was old and feeble and traveled the two blocks back and forth to Independence Hall in a sedan chair carried by four prisoners from the Walnut Street jail.

The roads were muddy, and it was two weeks before enough delegates arrived to make a quorum so that business could begin. Many delegates were also members of Congress, which was meeting in New York. Delegates would drift between New York and Philadelphia all summer, a two-day journey by public coach, with a stop overnight in Princeton.

Two of Georgia's delegates came down from Congress in May. The other two had to travel 800 miles from Georgia, the most distant state. Georgian Abraham Baldwin probably came the whole distance overland by public coach.

For some it was easier to get on a ship and sail the ocean to Philadelphia than to tackle the rough roads, mountains and bridgeless rivers — not to mention the threat of robbers and the certainty of bad food and bedbugs at many roadside inns.

Pierce Butler and Charles Cotesworth Pinckney of South Carolina came by sea.

Most of the delegates had to spend their own money for the privilege of getting to and staying in hot, sticky Philadelphia for three months.

The last delegate, John Francis Mercer of Maryland, didn't arrive until Aug. 6.

© Helen I. Driggs, 1987
James Madison

What if:

☛ Your country were ruled by a king?

☛ You couldn't go visit another state because people there used a different kind of money, a kind you didn't have and couldn't get?

☛ There were no super highways?

☛ Your country had no army or navy?

☛ There were no taxes?

☛ New York City declared itself the 51st state?

☛ Food raised in another state was being taxed in your state, so you couldn't afford to buy it?

☛ You were allowed to read whatever you wanted in your own state, and talk about it, but if you went to the state next door, you could be arrested for saying what you thought?

☛ Everything west of Ohio was another country, or perhaps four or five different countries?

These are a few of the things that could have happened if we had ended up with no Constitution, or a different one.

Some of these issues were already causing trouble in the 13 states at the time of the Constitutional Convention in 1787. Some of them went hand in hand.

Before the Constitution, Congress couldn't raise any money by taxes, so it couldn't pay for a real army or navy — or even pay off the country's debts.

A new country, in debt, not able to defend itself. That looked like easy pickings to older countries across the Atlantic Ocean.

Between the states there were problems, too. States were taxing each other's goods. They were using different kinds of money. It was difficult to move things over long distances.

The Constitution gives the federal government the right — and the obligation — to make money and to maintain a postal system and national highways. It forbids the states to tax each other's goods.

The Constitution limits the powers of the individual states in other ways.

For instance, it allows for the creation of new states, but it says that new states may *not* be made up from parts of old states, or by states joining with each other, unless they have permission from Congress and from the existing state or states.

So New York City could not become the 51st state (although New Yorkers suggest it from time to time) without congressional approval and the OK of the folks upstate.

The Constitution also protects the people. It says that citizens of any one state shall enjoy all the "privileges and immunities" of people in all the other states. So you couldn't have freedom of speech in one state and not in another, under our Constitution.

And you won't see a king in the United States under our Constitution either, although the possibility of a king of America was very real in 1787. That may seem surprising, when the colonies had just fought for eight years to get rid of a king. But people were used to the general idea. It had worked (most of the time) for years and years in England, France and elsewhere.

Hardly any delegates favored having a king, though. In the end, they decided we'd have an elected president instead, because the citizens would have more control over him.

The makers of the Constitution also tried to foresee the future. If they hadn't outlined a way for new states to be admitted to the union, it's possible that the United States would have stopped growing right where it was in 1787.

And because they couldn't predict the future, they also provided for amendments so that the Constitution could be changed. In fact, many delegates agreed to work immediately to get the first 10 amendments, called the Bill of Rights, adopted, and they were in 1791.

But the delegates didn't want changes to come too easily. Over the years, hundreds of amendments have been proposed to the Constitution, but since 1791, only 16 have been adopted.

DATELINE 1787

Sites and sounds of the city's past

Independence Hall

Chestnut Street between Fifth and Sixth Streets. Open 9 a.m. to 5 p.m. daily. 627-1776. Free.

Philadelphians called the State House, now Independence Hall, the "greatest ornament in town." But it was hot in the summer, cold and drafty in the winter. During the Constitutional Convention, 81-year-old Benjamin Franklin complained that the "unentertaining" echoes tired him out.

It was here that the Declaration of Independence was signed in 1776, even though the signers knew that if the war for liberty failed, they would be hanged. Here, in 1787, the Constitution was debated. The debaters knew that if they failed, there might never be a United States of America.

The State House wasn't at its best in the summer of 1787. The bell tower steeple had weakened and been torn down in 1781. In those days, they didn't build scaffolding to hold it up. They just tore it down.

There was construction all around, as the work began on Sixth Street for a new county courthouse, and on Fifth Street for the future home of Ben Franklin's pet project, the Philosophical Society.

There was the noise of hammering and the rumble of carts to contend with. Gravel was spread out front on Chestnut Street to quiet the noise of traffic. Piles of lumber blocked the streets.

It must have been stifling inside with doors and windows closed to preserve secrecy.

Across Walnut Street, looking directly into the State House yard, was the stone prison. Delegates and others passing by would be yelled at by prisoners who stuck their caps out on the end of long poles and cursed anyone who didn't drop money in.

The convention met daily in the east room from 10 a.m. until 3 or 4 p.m. Here you can see the way things looked: the long tables with green baize covers, the original "rising sun" chair where Washington sat when he was presiding, and the kind of quill pens and inkstands the delegates would have used, including the actual one used to sign the Constitution.

Across the hall is the Pennsylvania Supreme Court Chamber, with its prisoner's dock and jury boxes. Upstairs are the Governor's Council chambers and the Long Gallery, a long, narrow room where great public events were celebrated with dinners and dancing.

From the windows on the second floor you can see Independence Mall with its double row of 13 brick archways, and 13 flagpoles flying the flags of the original states.

ON THE SPOT

In the east room where the delegates met, there are a number of inkwells of the kind used at the time of the convention. See if you can find the one that was used to sign the Declaration of Independence and the Constitution, a beautiful silver inkstand designed by Philip Syng, a prominent Philadelphia silversmith, who also assisted Ben Franklin in his electrical experiments.

Notice the steps as you walk up to the Long Gallery. Why are they so worn? Would steps in a modern building get worn down this way? Why or why not?

Another treasure of Independence Hall is the "rising sun" chair. When the convention began, Ben Franklin wondered whether the sun was rising or setting. Why did he wonder that? What would we tell him today?

We think of graffiti as a modern problem — people writing on walls of buildings and other places. Can you find the graffiti carved (probably by workmen) on the wall of the stair landing in Independence Hall? What is its date?

☛*Answers: The Syng inkwell is on the Speaker's desk.*

The steps in Independence Hall are not the originals, but they get walked on by thousands of feet every year. They have a center portion called a stretcher that can be replaced so the whole step doesn't get torn out. A modern building would probably have concrete steps, or an elevator.

Franklin was worried about the real danger that the United States might not survive. Today we could tell him: So far, so good.

The date of the graffiti appears to be 1798.

THE HISTORIC MILE

The Syng Inkwell

Carpenters' Hall

320 Chestnut St. Open 10 a.m. to 4 p.m. Tuesday through Sunday. Free. 925-0167.

If you were a carpenter in Philadelphia at the time of the Constitutional Convention, you probably belonged to the Carpenters' Company. That was where you got ideas about building and even advice on how much to charge for your work.

If you were hurt on the job, the company helped pay your bills.

The Carpenters started building their hall in 1770 but didn't finish until 1774. The First Continental Congress used it for meetings. During the Revolution, the building was used as a military center.

During the Constitutional Convention, the Carpenters were responsible for much of that construction noise that bothered the delegates up the block at Independence Hall.

The Carpenters were not only responsible for the wooden parts of buildings (frames and floors and such). They were a powerful trade association because they had a secret price list that helped them estimate the cost of building, and through it, they controlled the other trade groups by acting as middlemen.

If you wanted something built, you would get the Carpenters to estimate the cost. Then they would hire the other trades — bricklayers, for instance — to help. When a member of the company died, his widow was required to return his copy of the price list to the company.

Building was done by hand, digging with a pick and shovel. Dirt was hauled away by horse and wagon. All work, from cutting down the trees to sawing boards to finishing the woodwork, was done with hand tools.

Examples of them can be seen in the display case in the lobby of the hall.

ON THE SPOT

A tool called a divider, which we would call a compass, was very basic to the carpenters' work — so much so that they used it as their trademark, or symbol. Can you find six examples of the divider in their hall?

Today's construction industry has many labor-saving devices. Can you name some of them? Can you find examples in Carpenters' Hall of the tools or the work that these devices have replaced?

☛*Answers: The dividers can be seen in the floor of the lobby and on banners inside the hall; a real one is in the lobby showcase.*

Today's construction relies on backhoes, power shovels, bucket loaders, cranes and a host of power hand tools — saws, drills, screwdrivers and more.

The Most Historic Mile

The area around Independence Hall has been called the most historic square mile in America. It includes all kinds of buildings that were in use in 1787 and can still be seen today. There are homes, churches, government and public buildings — even gardens.

This is where the delegates to the Constitutional Convention worked, lived, ate together and debated the future for more than three months in the summer of 1787. There are also museums where you can look into the way people lived, conducted business, played and fought.

A good place to get started looking at history is actually a rather new building — the Visitor Center, on Third Street between Chestnut and Walnut Streets.

The Visitor Center has maps, tickets and information about places to visit in Independence National Historical Park, the center of the historic area.

It offers a 28-minute film, *Independence,* which introduces you to some of the key men and women of the time — including drafters of the Declaration of Independence and, later, the Constitution.

In the Visitor Center's museum shop, you can find copies of toys that actually were used in early America.

The Visitor Center is open 9 a.m. to 5 p.m. daily. The phone number is 597-8974.

CONSTITUTIONAL QUIZ 1

1. The Constitutional Convention was held under conditions that are probably impossible today. True or false?
2. Why did the people from Europe, called colonists, come to this country to live?
   a. Some came for religious and political freedom.
   b. Some came to trade.
   c. Some came to teach the native Indians.
   d. All of the above.
3. What reason was *not* given by the colonists for declaring themselves free from Great Britain?
   a. The colonists were required to pay taxes on goods from other countries.
   b. The colonists were not represented in Parliament.
   c. British soldiers searched homes illegally for goods without tax stamps.
   d. British soldiers stayed in colonists' homes without the owners' approval.
4. For a time it was proposed that only property owners should hold public office. True or false?

(Answers: Page 75)

© Helen I. Driggs, 1987

Old City Hall

Southwest corner, Fifth and Chestnut Streets. Open 9 a.m. to 5 p.m. daily. Free. 597-8974.

It was, and still is, the task of the Supreme Court to determine the meaning of the Constitution. Old City Hall was the meeting place of the U.S. Supreme Court from 1791 to 1800.

The building we call Old City Hall wasn't known that way in 1787. In fact, it wasn't even built. It was authorized in 1789 and was built in the next two years.

A two-story brick building with a peaked roof topped by a cupola, it stands beside Independence Hall. It was the center of city government for about 100 years, until the present City Hall was built.

Old City Hall eventually became a museum. The chamber used by the Supreme Court has just finished being restored to approximate its original appearance.

While the Supreme Court of the United States was meeting in its borrowed space in City Hall, the mayor of Philadelphia was in the room next door, conducting the city's business.

City Tavern

Second and Walnut Streets. Open 11:30 a.m. to 11 p.m. daily. 923-6059.

"September 17, 1787: The business being closed, the members adjourned to the City Tavern. . . ."
— *George Washington's diary*

Want the latest news? Need to buy a cargo of goods from Europe? Organize your own company? Read the newspaper just in from London? Hear a concert? Give a dance? Hold a club meeting?

If you lived in Philadelphia 200 years ago and wanted to do any of those things, there were many taverns in town you could go to, but the best one was City Tavern. It was an elegant social and business center. John Adams called it "America's most genteel tavern."

Much of the conversation was about politics, and City Tavern was a familiar spot to the delegates throughout the convention, not just at the end. In fact, two of the out-of-towners were staying there — Dr. William Samuel Johnson of Connecticut and Rufus King of Massachusetts.

Out-of-towners rented rooms on the third floor, at $6 a night. Guests could buy drinks and snacks. Dinner was usually eaten about 3 p.m.

The City Tavern you see now is only 11 years old, built on the site to look just like the original, which was demolished about 150 years ago. Like the other buildings in Independence Park, it is owned by the U.S. government.

City Tavern is an operating restaurant. The staff wears colonial costumes, and the menu offers food that is like what people might have eaten in 1787: pheasant, quail, duck, fish. (But it is surely cooked to be more tasty than the Founding Fathers' food.) There's a bar, too.

People who don't want to eat or drink are invited in anyway to take a look.

PATHWAY TO THE CONSTITUTION

B. It will take more than a month for the convention actually to agree to the plan, but in the end, it produces the legislative branch as we know it. Sherman goes down in history as the man who saved the day with his Connecticut Compromise.

6. Aug. 6, 1787: North and South begin to wrestle over how to determine population. The larger a state's population, the more power it will have. The debate will go on most of this month.

a. You are going to vote with James Wilson of Pennsylvania. All whites and "other free citizens" will count as one person each. Indians won't count at all. "All other persons" will count as three-fifths of a person each.

b. You stand with the Southern states: Slaves will be counted as people. That will increase Southern states' population and give them more power.

c. You stand with the North: It is outrageous for Southern states to claim slaves as people when they treat slaves as property. Slaves should not be counted at all for congressional representation.

d. You believe the Constitution should abolish slavery and then count everyone for government representation.

(What did the Constitution Framers decide? Go to Page 61.)

Congress Hall

Sixth and Chestnut Streets. Open 9 a.m. to 5 p.m. daily; during the summer, open 9 a.m. to 6 p.m. daily. Free. 597-8974.

Six dollars a day! That's what the members of the Senate and House of Representatives were paid *if* they attended the sessions of the first Congress. And they paid their own expenses while living away from home, too. The Senate met upstairs in Congress Hall, the House downstairs, kept warm by six fireplaces on each floor.

But that was after the Constitution was ratified, or approved, by all the states. In 1787, work on Congress Hall had just begun — except at that time, everybody thought it would be the Philadelphia county courthouse.

But it was finished in 1789, just in time for it to be volunteered for the new Congress of the United States. Philadelphia in 1790 was the capital of the United States and of the Commonwealth of Pennsylvania. It was also the county seat. Four levels of government were all operating at once in the same place. That has never happened in this country since then.

Maybe the delegates weren't paid much, but we know they enjoyed some luxury when they met — mahogany tables, carpeting, Franklin stoves in the fireplaces and Venetian blinds in the windows.

George Washington's second term as president began here in 1793 with the swearing-in. But the eyes of the world watched more closely at the end of that term.

Would Washington really give up power after eight years? Could the new government of the United States manage the transfer of power to a second president without the whole system falling apart?

We know the answer now, but nobody was sure of it then.

ON THE SPOT

Can you find the Franklin stoves in the fireplaces on the first floor? Do they look like a wood stove you might see today? Why do you think they represented an improvement over plain fireplaces?

Look for the inkwell slots in the tables on the first floor, where the House of Representatives met. Can you guess why each slot is divided into three sections?

☛*Answers: Benjamin Franklin designed his metal fireplace inserts, which were dubbed "stoves," to improve heating. They retain and radiate heat, making the fireplace more efficient.*

The three desk slots contained an inkwell full of ink, quill pens and sand — to be scattered on written papers to help the ink dry.

The Liberty Bell

Independence Mall, near Fifth and Market Streets. Open 9 a.m. to 5 p.m. daily; during the summer, open 9 a.m. to 8 p.m. daily. Free. When pavilion is closed, bell is visible through the glass walls. 627-1776.

At the end of Independence Mall is the Liberty Bell Pavilion, the glass-and-steel building that has housed the Liberty Bell since 1976. Around the top of the bell are words from the Bible: "Proclaim liberty thoughout all the land unto all the inhabitants thereof."

The 2,080-pound bell did just that in the early life of the United States and is said to have rung at such important events as the proclamation of the Declaration of Independence in 1776.

The time-honored story is that it cracked while tolling in 1835 for the funeral of the fourth chief justice of the United States, John Marshall, and that the crack was extended in 1846 when the bell was struck to celebrate the anniversary of the birth of George Washington.

The Liberty Bell is unique in another way: You won't find a "keep away" sign sign on it. You're welcome to go right up and touch it.

YELLOW FEVER

In 1793, Old City Hall became the center of the fight to deal with a citywide emergency: yellow fever. The city was dirty. Outhouses were built near wells, which provided drinking water. Garbage was thrown into the streets. Rats were everywhere. Nobody understood that sickness and sanitation were related.

In 1793, 4,000 people in Philadelphia died, and 20,000 moved out of the city into the country. The sick, the dying, the dead lay in the streets. Many people believed (wrongly) that black people could not catch yellow fever, and many black people helped with the sick when the mayor put out the call for volunteers.

Richard Allen and Absalom Jones, both outstanding black church leaders, were among the brave and tireless volunteers.

Portrait Statue of George Washington

BEN FRANKLIN MR. EVERYTHING

A man whose genius outlives him

Franklin Court

314-322 Market St. 9 a.m. to 5 p.m. daily, except 10 a.m. to 6 p.m. June 29 through Sept. 5. Free. 597-2761.

Benjamin Franklin was an extraordinary man. He had only two years of formal education, in grammar school. But he became a printer who wrote, published and printed his own newspaper and almanac, and he established the first lending library.

He organized a firefighting company and set up the first fire-insurance company. He helped found a university and a hospital. He was a postmaster who improved postal services among the 13 colonies. He experimented with electricity and invented a lightning rod.

What's a better way to pave, clean and light 18th-century streets? Ben figured it all out. He improved fireplaces with his Franklin stove, and he designed furniture, musical instruments and bifocal eyeglasses. He felt that women should be educated and that college should be free to anyone who passed the exams.

Ben Franklin had no money when he came to Philadelphia from Boston as a teenager. But by age 42 he was rich, so he retired from work to spend the rest of his life serving his country.

He spent many years in London, where he represented the colonies in their complaints against British rule. He was a delegate to the Second Continental Congress, which issued the Declaration of Independence, and he was ambassador to France during the Revolutionary War.

When he was 81, he took part in the Constitutional Convention. Three weeks before he died in 1790, he wrote a paper asking the United States to abolish slavery.

In 1762, Ben planned a home for his wife and family, right down to the color of paint he wanted for each room. But he was abroad for so many years that his wife, Deborah, was responsible for completing the construction. Later, Ben added to the main house, built three tenant houses and built a print shop for his grandson.

Franklin's home was torn down in 1812, and when it came time to try to evoke or re-create his lifestyle, there was no remaining picture of how his house looked. So it was decided to erect a steel frame to show us roughly how and where the house stood.

The rest of the courtyard has stones inscribed with quotes from letters between Ben and Deborah, written as the building of the house progressed. You can also peer down into spots where foundations of the house or its outbuildings have been excavated.

Beneath the courtyard is an underground museum. In the Dimension Room, flashing neon lights spell out the eight categories that describe Benjamin Franklin: inventor, statesman, author, citizen, diplomat, printer, publisher, scientist. Franklin would have loved the neon.

In the museum, you can see an original Franklin stove, as well as some of Franklin's other inventions: bifocals, an air pump used in electrical experiments and an insulating stool he used during the experiments to avoid electrical shocks.

Franklin made up much of the language we use to talk about electricity today, including *electrode* and *plus* and *minus*, which had been used before the 1700s to talk about numbers, but not about electricity.

In the museum, there is a reproduction of his "library chair," a chair that has a built-in ladder to use in getting to books on high shelves. Portraits of his family include one of his son Frankie, who died at age 4, and one of a favorite grandson, William Temple Franklin, who went to France with Ben.

ON THE SPOT

In the museum's telephone room, lift up one of the telephones and dial 278-52-18 to hear what Mme. A. L. Brillon says causes all women to love Ben Franklin. Or dial any of the 46 other men and women, American and European, to find out their opinions of him.

On the opposite side of the room, push 07 and read what Ben says is "The Secret of Keeping a Secret." Lots of other amusing and wise sayings can be called up at the push of a button.

Watch a sound-and-light show play out three dramatic scenes in Franklin's life: facing the British government in 1776, the French court in 1778 and the Constitutional Convention in 1787.

In the print shop, which turns out items you can buy, you can see an 18th-century printing press at work. Go to the real working post office on the site to buy a card and stamp so you can ask for the "B. Free Franklin" postmark.

BEN FRANKLIN MR. EVERYTHING

“

Early to bed and early to rise, makes a man healthy, wealthy, and wise.

When the well's dry, we know the worth of water.

Little strokes, fell great oaks.

Remember that time is money.

. . . snug as a bug in a rug.

Eat not to dullness; drink not to elevation.

Three may keep a secret, if two of them are dead.

Necessity never made a good bargain.

Keep your eyes wide open before marriage, half shut afterwards.

The used key is always bright

A word to the wise is enough, and many words won't fill a bushel.

A cat in gloves catches no mice.

And this, in a letter written in 1789:

Our Constitution is in actual operation; everything appears to promise that it will last; but in this world nothing is certain but death and taxes.

”

The American Philosophical Society

104 S. Fifth St. Open 9 a.m. to 5 p.m. Monday through Friday. Free. 627-0706.

Fifteen signers of the Constitution were members of the American Philosophical Society. The society and the Library Company were just two of busy Ben Franklin's many projects.

Franklin started the society in 1743 to “improve the common stock of knowledge.” But for more than 25 years, there weren't enough people of education around with time to attend meetings.

By the time of the Constitutional Convention, however, the society was building its own hall in Independence Square. The two-story brick building, known as Philosophical Hall, faces its companion building, Library Hall, across Fifth Street.

There was no “science” in those days, and no “technology” as we know it. The members gathered knowledge of all sorts, but they were especially interested in practical improvements. What's a better way to build windmills? Calculate longitude? Get oil from sunflower seeds?

The society was a library, a museum, a place of knowledge. It has been publishing its findings since before the Revolution.

Members are elected on the basis of their achievements. The first woman joined in 1789. She was a Russian princess who was president of the Imperial Academy of Sciences.

Both Franklin and Thomas Jefferson were presidents of the society.

The society's library, on the original location of the Library Company of Philadelphia at 105 S. Fifth St., has two small exhibits each year in the lobby.

Benjamin Franklin made a good deal of his fortune as a writer and a publisher. His Poor Richard's Almanac was a favorite with the colonists for almost 30 years, beginning in the 1730s, and was full of pithy sayings. He wrote them elsewhere, too. Some sayings that are a part of our everyday life were made up by Franklin. Others that he made up have been modified over the years and have become commonplace in a different form. Still others may not be well-known, but certainly should be:

PONDER THIS

Why do you think the Contributionship had the rule about trees?

☛ Answer: Trees made it harder to get the pumper near the house. Also, it was feared that they sometimes would draw lightning.

CONSTITUTION QUIZ 2

1. When is the president officially elected?
2. The Constitutional Convention did not have a chaplain because the Founding Fathers didn't want to mix politics and religion. True or false?
3. How did people originally delegate authority to the federal government?
    a. They voted for presidential electors.
    b. They paid state taxes.
    c. They accepted the Constitution.
    d. They amended the Constitution.
4. Soldiers of a Pennsylvania army regiment once took the Continental Congress hostage. True or false?
5. If we had kept the original ratio of representation in the House of Representatives, how many members would we now have?

(Answers: Page 75)

BEN FRANKLIN MR. EVERYTHING

BEN FRANKLIN MR. EVERYTHING

The Franklin Institute

20th Street and the Benjamin Franklin Parkway. Open 10 a.m. to 5 p.m. Monday through Saturday, and noon to 5 p.m. Sunday. Admission: adults, $4.50; children 4 to 11, $3.50; senior citizens, $3; children under 4, free. 448-1200.

The Franklin Institute, founded in 1824, will give you the *real* story about the kite Franklin flew in a thunderstorm.

It will also show you a lot of things that Franklin would probably love to have seen, since science is its focus. There is an enormous amount to see *and* do here, sights and sounds, trains and planes — even a planetarium. This is a museum that no child (no matter how old) should miss.

Franklin wistfully said he had been "born out of time," because he felt that the world was on the brink of many great discoveries he would not live to see. He wished he could live 200 years after his time.

And here we are, 200 years later, and the new exhibit at the institute is called "Born Out of Time." It celebrates Franklin's achievements.

The threat of fire

Fireman's Hall Museum. Second Street, between Arch and Race. Open 9 a.m. to 5 p.m. Tuesday through Saturday. Free. 923-1438.

The Philadelphia Contributionship. 212 S. Fourth St. By appointment. Free. 627-1752.

The Mutual Assurance Co. 240 S. Fourth St. Open 8:30 a.m. to 5 p.m. Monday through Friday. Free. 925-0609.

Cigna Corp. 16th and Arch Streets. Open 7:45 a.m. to 5 p.m. Monday through Friday. Free. 557-5000.

When the cry "Fire!" was heard, everyone ran to the scene with buckets. Women passed empty buckets; men passed full ones. Water from the buckets was poured into the pumper, which was run by the volunteer fire brigade. It took six men to operate. The spray reached 30 to 40 feet.

There were no hydrants, hoses or helmets — and no fire engine as we know them. Horse-drawn fire engines hadn't even come on the scene yet.

This was 1787.

But no one understood the danger of city fire better than William Penn, the father of Philadelphia, who founded the city more than a century earlier.

Penn had witnessed the terrible destruction caused by the Great London Fire of 1666, which had left almost nothing standing. That's partly why he laid out *his* city with wide streets (harder for the fire to jump) and open spaces.

But it was Ben Franklin who got firefighting and fire prevention organized in Philadelphia.

Franklin organized the first volunteer fire company in 1736. He wrote articles about fire prevention. He was a founder of the oldest fire insurance company in the nation, The Philadelphia Contributionship for the Insurance of Houses From Loss by Fire. Founded in 1752, **The Philadelphia Contributionship** is still going strong at 212 S. Fourth St.

The city had some fire laws. The Contributionship had its rules, too: no insurance for wood houses; no insurance if a shade tree was too close to a house.

The company adopted a "firemark," a small plaque that would be displayed on a house that was insured. It was supposed to encourage quick action in case of fire because the volunteer fire brigades got money from the Contributionship to support their work.

It also encouraged other people who were insured by the company to help put out a fire. Less damage meant lower insurance rates for everybody.

Contributionship "hand-in-hand" firemarks can still be seen on old houses.

A rival fire insurance group, the Mutual Assurance Co., defied Franklin's company with its rule about cutting down trees by the house. Established in 1784, it adopted the picture of a tree for its firemark.

Fire gear, firemarks, old uniforms and pumpers and much more can be seen at **Fireman's Hall Museum**. It also has a remarkable stained-glass portrayal of a fire scene. The hall originally housed Engine Company No. 8, the direct descendant of Franklin's first volunteers.

At the Contributionship, you can see more fire gear and some of the company's most valued papers, including surveys of Franklin's house and Carpenters' Hall, which the Contributionship still insures.

Other collections of fire gear can be seen at the **Mutual Assurance Co.** and at **Cigna Corp.**

PATHWAY TO THE CONSTITUTION

C. The delegates agreed with John Dickinson of Delaware that the states should not be dissolved but that they already *were* a nation, like it or not, and had better be a strong one.

3. June 1, 1787: Who is going to lead the country? No one has yet mentioned the word *president.* Charles Pinckney of South Carolina suggests a "chief executive."

a. You vote no, because a single leader will mean having a king.

b. You agree with Edmund Randolph of Virginia that the "executive" should be a committee of three, instead of one man.

c. You agree with Pierce Butler of South Carolina: Having three men will confuse people and weaken the government. You join George Washington and others in voting "aye" ("yes") for one chief executive.

d. You vote "no" because, as Alexander Hamilton suggested, you think the United States should have a king.

(What did the Constitution Framers decide? Go to Page 69.)

BEN FRANKLIN MR. EVERYTHING

The main man came to work, but many heroes stayed away

Surprisingly, some of the great names of the Revolution were missing when it came time to invent a nation's government. The greatest one of them all almost didn't make it.

☛ George Washington *was* there. He didn't want to come. He had rheumatism. He loved his Virginia home, Mount Vernon, and was tired of always being called away. At 55, he was no longer young. In February 1787 he wrote to a friend, war hero Henry Knox, about the convention set for May in Philadelphia: "It is not at this time my purpose to attend it." But he was persuaded at last that the American people would not accept the convention without his name at the head of it. In fact, his name meant so much that many of the delegates did not decide to come until they heard that Washington had arrived in Philadelphia. He presided.

☛ Benjamin Franklin, the well-loved Philadelphian — inventor, writer, patriot, ambassador, genius of his time — was, at 81, the oldest delegate. He kept tempers cool with his wisdom and sense of humor.

☛ Alexander Hamilton, who had fought at Washington's side in the war, was there from New York. He worked at the convention, but his efforts were most important afterward, when he was one of the writers of the Federalist Papers. His brilliant arguments helped persuade the states to ratify, or approve, the Constitution that the delegates had drawn up.

☛ James Madison of Virginia was only 5-foot-6 and very thin, but he was one of the giants among the Founding Fathers. In fact, he was known as the "Father of the Constitution," and he took notes every day of the convention. The delegates knew he could be trusted to tell no one what he was writing, and the notes, so important today in helping us to understand what went on, weren't published until after his death. In 1809, he became the fourth U.S. president.

Among the missing — two future presidents and two other great patriots:

☛ Thomas Jefferson, author of the Declaration of Independence, one day to be the third U.S. president, was serving as ambassador to France. He was very excited about the convention and flooded the delegates with books that he thought might be helpful, sending them in crates on ships across the Atlantic from Paris. He was not entirely happy when he learned how strong the Constitution would be in establishing a national government and that it did not have a bill of rights. The first 10 amendments, known as the Bill of Rights, were not adopted until 1791.

☛ John Adams, signer of the Declaration of Independence and the future second U.S. president, was ambassador to England. From London, he supported the convention with a book he had written defending the need for a Constitution.

☛ Patrick Henry ("Give me liberty or give me death") stayed home in Virginia. The convention sounded like too much government and not enough liberty. He said he "smelt a rat."

☛ Tom Paine ("These are the times that try men's souls") was in England on business.

Also, one whole delegation was missing. Rhode Island, the smallest state in the union, feared losing all of its power to the big states and refused to attend.

The Library Company of Philadelphia

1314 Locust St. Open 9 a.m. to 4:45 p.m. Monday through Friday. Free. 546-3181.

What was on the shelves of the Library Company at the time the delegates were writing the Constitution? place. Books that set forth political ideas, old and new. Books the delegates pondered.

Books they borrowed — and didn't return on time. The overdue notices prove it.

The Library Company, another brainchild of Ben Franklin's, was the country's first circulating library, one that allowed people to borrow books and take them home. It was a very democratic idea, in an age when books were rare, expensive and almost impossible to get. And remember, in an era before movies, TV, magazines or radio, books were a major form of entertainment as well as education.

The original Library Company was located at Library Hall, 105 S. Fifth St. The building there now, erected in 1959 to look like Library Hall, is occupied by the library of the American Philosophical Society.

At its Locust Street address today, the Library Company carries on the work that Franklin began, as a major research library for American history, science, medicine and architecture. Its museum is open to the public at 1314 Locust.

PONDER THIS

The first "men of science" were wealthy, educated gentlemen who didn't need to work for a living. What qualifications does a scientist need today?

Detail of an 18th-Century Embroidered Sampler

Turning back the clock to 1787

Why did people come to Philadelphia? It was the biggest, most important, most central city in the colonies. Philadelphia welcomed immigrants, who stayed because of the freedom, because of the rich farm land and because of the many opportunities to better themselves.

When America was just the 13 colonies, overseas trade was brisk. Food, furs and lumber were sold to other countries. Rum and sugar from the West Indies and goods made in England were bought from them.

After independence, the former colonies were cut out of trade with England. Philadelphia reflected the hard times after the Revolution. Visitors saw peeling paint, abandoned houses, homes destroyed in the war that were not yet being rebuilt.

In 1787, the city was just pulling out of its postwar slump. The first Philadelphia ship to China, the Canton, had just sailed. Of course, it would take months to get there and to return. But the "China trade" would make some merchants wealthy in the 1790s.

Like any city, Philadelphia had its rich and its poor. The rich left many things behind, so we know a lot about how they lived.

The poor might be unable to afford even a single pot to cook in. Their rickety wooden houses, often with wooden chimneys, burned or fell down in time. They have not left us much of a record of their lives. Mostly we know what others wrote about them.

In between was a middle class that struggled to keep out of debt and maybe get ahead. In this class were the better craftsmen, called "masters." They might be tailors, potters, pewter makers, shoemakers, bakers or blacksmiths. The silversmiths were usually members of the wealthy class.

Craftsmen worked in their homes, with perhaps a helper (an apprentice or journeyman) who was learning the job. There was no big business. If there was a big job to be done, people were brought together for their specific skills — the way the Carpenters' Company hired crews to build.

Local trade took place in general stores, at a few specialty shops such as apothecaries or bookstores, at fairs or markets, and through peddlers. Philadelphia was famous for its street sellers, among them oyster women and fishwives selling the fish their husbands caught.

The farmers' markets that were held three days a week on High Street attracted people from all over. They sold every sort of fresh food — meat, too, from animals that were slaughtered right on the spot. Of course there were no refrigerators, and no tin cans either.

The markets were so important that people stopped calling the street High Street and it became known by the name it has today, Market Street.

Candles, made from beef fat or beeswax, were costly and were used only when necessary. Light came from the fireplace, which also provided the only heat in the house.

Most people owned no more than two sets of clothing. Women knitted stockings and mittens. There were no special clothes for cold weather. People just added layers.

Little girls made samplers, which taught them both the alphabet and sewing stitches.

Reading, writing and arithmetic were learned at home, often with the Bible as the only book. George Washington had only a grade-school education. In the cities, sons from wealthy families might go to private schools or have tutors. Books published for children taught manners, courtesy and obedience.

In Philadelphia, people could attend plays, concerts, poetry readings and light opera. Auctions were popular. If you enjoyed reading, you could borrow a book from the Library Company. Everybody loved horse racing. Just as Market Street eventually took its name from what went on there, so Race Street got that name from the horse racing along it.

Fishing was popular along the Delaware. (Remember, the Schuylkill, Philadelphia's other big river, was still way out in the woods before 1800, when nobody lived past about Seventh Street.)

In winter, ice skating on the Delaware was a favorite pastime. In those days, when the water was much more pure than it is today, the big river would freeze over when the temperatures dropped into the middle 20s for a few days. Now the river is too polluted to turn to ice at temperatures so near to 32 degrees.

City folk could buy fabric and have their clothes made for them — if they could afford it. Wealthy people gave balls, fancy dances with real orchestras. The women copied European fashions for their gowns and accessories.

Visiting was an important part of social life. Because transportation was difficult, people coming from far away usually stayed a long time. Christmas was a quiet religious holiday. Gift-giving and feasting took place on New Year's Day.

Visitors from Europe were surprised by the openness of society. The seven weekly newspapers in Philadelphia at the time of independence were read and discussed by almost everybody. Since each was published on a different day of the week, it was like having a daily paper.

The businesses that made men rich were banking, the merchant (or import-export) business and real estate. Buying undeveloped land in the vast wilderness that made up most of the country was a good way to make a fortune — and lose it. Philadelphian Robert Morris, a

(Continued on next page)

(Continued from preceding page)
Constitutional Convention delegate, was a man of wealth and importance in 1787 — one of the richest in the nation. In 1798, his real estate deals had gone sour and landed him in debtors' prison.

For most people, life was not so dramatic. Working-class folk might hope to own a little house and live comfortably — if they were lucky, and if husband and wife had some skilled trade, and if they stayed healthy and if their children lived to help them or get work as apprentices. For unskilled laborers, a day of work meant food on the table for that day. No work meant no food. For them, there was no such thing as a regular "job."

Within Philadelphia's "historic mile," the people who owned houses were pretty well-to-do. In an age of no public transportation, the center of the city was the best place to live. Several houses have been restored to tell us how some city folk lived.

As more and more people came to Philadelphia, more and more houses were built to shelter them. Eighty percent of the homes were rented out by their owners to others. The owners paid taxes based on the number of feet that fronted the street. That is why so many of the old houses are very narrow and long.

Craftsmen from Holland and Germany introduced glazed brick and Flemish-bond brick patterns. That is one way you can identify old buildings.

Trinity houses were built for working people. They're sometimes called Father, Son and Holy Ghost houses or faith, hope and charity houses. They are small — three square or rectangular rooms set one on top of each other, with a winding staircase going from floor to floor.

The houses were made of brick, with wooden floors. There was no separate kitchen in these houses. Cooking was done in the fireplace.

To see four trinities, look for Bingham Court on St. Joseph's Way, off Spruce between Third and Fourth Streets.

Wealthy people built larger, more elegant homes with formal gardens. There were no "architects" as we know the term. Building ideas were found at Carpenters' Hall. The master carpenters and other craftspeople of Philadelphia constructed some of the finest buildings in America.

There were no bathrooms. People used wash basins and tubs. Too much washing was thought to be dangerous, opening the pores to let in illness.

Educated city people slept with lots of pillows, almost sitting up in bed. They believed that lying down would make the blood go to the head and prevent them from waking up the next morning. This habit accounts in part for the beds being so short.

Wood-burning fireplaces kept people warm, and most homes had fire shields nearby. Why? Many people, men and women, had smallpox scars. They filled these holes with a cosmetic cream made mostly of wax. The shield protected the face so the wax wouldn't melt when they sat by the fire.

The delegates

The 55 delegates to the Constitutional Convention had a lot in common:

Most of them were well-educated. Some were self-taught; some had tutors. Half of them attended college.

Almost all of them were well-to-do. A few were rich.

They had experience in politics and were active in their communities.

Most had been involved in the Revolution.

Only seven were born outside the colonies.

Ten were bachelors, three were widowers. The rest were married, most of them with children.

Two were Catholics, and the rest were Protestants.

The youngest were in their late 20s. The oldest, Ben Franklin, was 81. The average age was 44.

They hated tyrants.

They believed in reason.

They wanted a government that belonged to the people.

They were all white and all male.

But the delegates differed in significant ways:

Some figured they'd profit as a result of a new constitution. Others knew they'd lose money.

Some hoped to get jobs in the new government.

Some were more ambitious than others.

Some lost their tempers easily; some were calm.

Some were friends; some were rivals.

They all had different ideas about what was best for their particular state.

Only 39 of them actually signed the Constitution.

In addition:

Eight had been together at Valley Forge, and 33 of them had served in the Revolutionary War.

Eight signed the Declaration of Independence.

Nine were Princeton graduates.

Eleven were business associates of Robert Morris.

Fourteen became U.S. senators.

Five served in the House of Representatives.

Five served on the Supreme Court.

Twelve were governors.

CONSTITUTION QUIZ 3

1. The expenses for the delegates to the Constitutional Convention were paid by each state. True or false?

2. What power is *not* delegated by the Constitution to the United States government?

a. The power to levy and collect taxes.

b. The power to create and maintain a postal service.

c. The power to offer an education to all citizens.

d. The power to make treaties.

3. Some states refused to accept the Constitution:

a. because they thought it was not fair.

b. because it did not have a Bill of Rights.

c. because they thought it was too long.

d. because they still wanted to be governed by England.

(Answers: Page 75)

LIFESTYLE 1787

Fashionable Clothing in 1787

Gone fishin': How Washington spent a summer vacation

When George Washington went anywhere in public, people gathered to watch the famous man, almost the way they would gather today around a movie or television star.

At the theater, they'd get more interested in him than the show. After he became president, they had a tendency to refer to him as "His Highness," even though he was clearly not a king.

So perhaps it's no wonder that when the Constitutional Convention adjourned in late July for a 10-day vacation, Washington took the opportunity to leave town.

During the convention, he was living at the home of fellow delegate Robert Morris, but he rode out of town with another delegate, Gouverneur Morris (no relation to Robert). They hitched Washington's horses to a light carriage that belonged to Gouverneur Morris and went fishing!

Washington told in his diary how they rented rooms overnight and the next day set out "in the vicinity of Valley Forge to get Trout." But while Morris was fishing, Washington couldn't resist the pull of a memory that was 10 years old.

He rode over to the fields where he and his men had spent the bitter winter of 1777-78, freezing, hungry and in rags. The defenses that he remembered were "in Ruins," and the fields were plowed under the hot July sun.

The next day it rained, and they went back to Philadelphia. But before the 10-day recess was over, Washington was off fishing again.

He escaped the city heat and crowds, and also a double bill at the city's opera house — a concert followed by a five-act comedy! The general had been known to fall asleep over less, and he was probably very pleased to be catching perch and touring Trenton instead.

Graff House

Seventh and Market Streets. Open 9 a.m. to 5 p.m. daily. Free. 597-8974.

At the northern end of the historic mile, toward the more working-class part of town, a bricklayer named Jacob Graff built himself a brick home in 1775. The original Graff House lasted more than 100 years, but it was eventually torn down in 1883, after serving as a printer's shop. The house was reconstructed in 1976 because it is remembered as the place where Thomas Jefferson wrote the Declaration of Independence.

(Jefferson would doubtless have loved to be present for the Constitutional Convention, but he was America's ambassador to France at the time. He did keep in touch, by mail, with the

When Jefferson wrote the Declaration of Independence, he was was just 33 years old. He wrote it without notes from June 11 to June 28, 1776. The Continental Congress then reviewed and debated it, sentence by sentence. They liked, respected and trusted Jefferson, even though he was the second-youngest of the delegates. He was a Virginian, a lawyer, scientist, farmer and student of history.

To have quiet and fresh air, he rented two rooms on the second floor of the house that bricklayer Graff had just finished building. Jefferson brought along the folding lap desk he had designed and the violin he loved to play.

Jefferson got up at dawn every day and soaked his feet in a pan of cold water. He believed that would keep him from catching cold.

PATHWAY TO THE CONSTITUTION

C. The compromise gave the North some trade arrangements it desperately wanted, for the Northern states depended on exporting and importing. The South got its slaves, but no more were to be imported after 1808. The compromise was the best the convention could do, and it wasn't all that good. It took the terrible Civil War 75 years later to settle the issue.

8. Aug. 20, 1787: Can "foreigners" be members of Congress? How long do you have to live here to become a citizen?

a. You decide that the president definitely must be born here, and that members of Congress should have lived here for a few years at least. You vote for seven years for the House of Representatives and nine for the Senate.

b. Gouverneur Morris says it takes seven years to become a shoemaker. It should take 14 to become a senator.

c. James Wilson, who was born in Scotland, reminds you that many patriots of *your* Revolution were "foreigners." Mason, Franklin, Alexander Hamilton (born in the West Indies) and you agree: Just being here should be enough!

d. You agree that a foreign-born person should be able to rise to any height, but that all candidates for public office should have lived here for 10 years.

(What did the Constitution Framers decide? Go to Page 55.)

Graff House
Helen I. Driggs, 1987

Marriage, family:
The highway of life might be full of curves and potholes

Life was certainly not always smooth for Philadelphians — especially women — in 1787.

There was no such thing as divorce. Husbands and wives sometimes went to court to resolve problems, or they just ran away from them.

Benjamin Franklin, for instance, never formally married his wife, Deborah. Before she knew Ben, she had been married to another man who had run away. Technically, she was married to that man all her life, but she became Franklin's "common law" wife by living with him. It was not an uncommon arrangement in those times.

Also, not surprisingly, children were born to women who were not married. Many of them became quite successful. Franklin had a son, William, with a woman who was not his wife. William lived with Ben and Deborah and eventually became governor of New Jersey. After he sided with Britain in the Revolution, however, he and his father stopped speaking to each other.

Alexander Hamilton, one of the most important Founding Fathers, was born on the Caribbean island of Nevis. His mother, Rachel Fawcett Lavien, was not married to his father, James Hamilton.

Usually families were very large. Ben Franklin had at least 12 brothers and sisters (the exact number is uncertain). Roger Sherman, the man who get credit for the most important compromise at the Constitutional Convention, had 15 children.

On the other hand, the rate of infant mortality, or death among little children, was very high. Well over half of all children in the city died before they were 2.

Women often had 10 children by their 30s, but many women also died in childbirth, and a child without a mother to nurse it had little hope of living. Children were welcome because their work helped the family get what was needed to stay alive and make money.

Women had few legal rights. They could own nothing. Their clothes belonged first to their fathers, then to their husbands. If a married woman inherited money, it belonged to her husband. If husband and wife separated, she had no place to go except back to her father. If she got a job, the money legally belonged to her husband. Even the children belonged to their father.

CONSTITUTION QUIZ 4

1. Which of these is *not* an objective of the United States Constitution, as stated in the Preamble?
   a. The federal government would have the power to defend all of the states.
   b. The country would be a better union of states.
   c. The government would work for the good of all people.
   d. The country would be free from the control of England.
2. Currently, there is one representative in the House for about every 521,000 citizens. Do states with fewer than 521,000 people not have a representative in Congress?
3. All 13 states were represented at the convention during the entire 16-week meeting. True or false?
4. At the beginning of the Constitutional Convention, it was rumored that the son of King George III would be made king of the United States. True or false?
5. Why did the Pennsylvania legislature rush to ratify the Constitution as quickly as possible?

(Answers: Page 75)

PATHWAY TO THE CONSTITUTION

D. The final decision was that nine states' approval would be needed. Each state was given the responsibility of choosing a state convention to ratify, but the delegates to the conventions were to be elected by the people, with approval of the state legislatures.

10. Sept. 12, 1787. Hold it! We need to be sure that our most precious rights, like trial by jury and freedom of the press, are included in the Constitution.

a. Right! You agree with George Mason. Lots of states have a Bill of Rights already. We could look at a few of them and put one together in a jiffy.

b. Nonsense! You agree with Roger Sherman. The states' Bills of Rights are enough. Leave well enough alone.

c. You think we can always have a Bill of Rights later. After all, what are amendments for? The Pennsylvania Assembly wants its room back. Let's sign this document and go home.

d. You'd rather keep arguing. Your summer in Philadelphia has been so much fun, you'd like to hang around and see what winter is like.

(What did the Constitution Framers decide? Go to Page 73.)

LIFESTYLE 1787

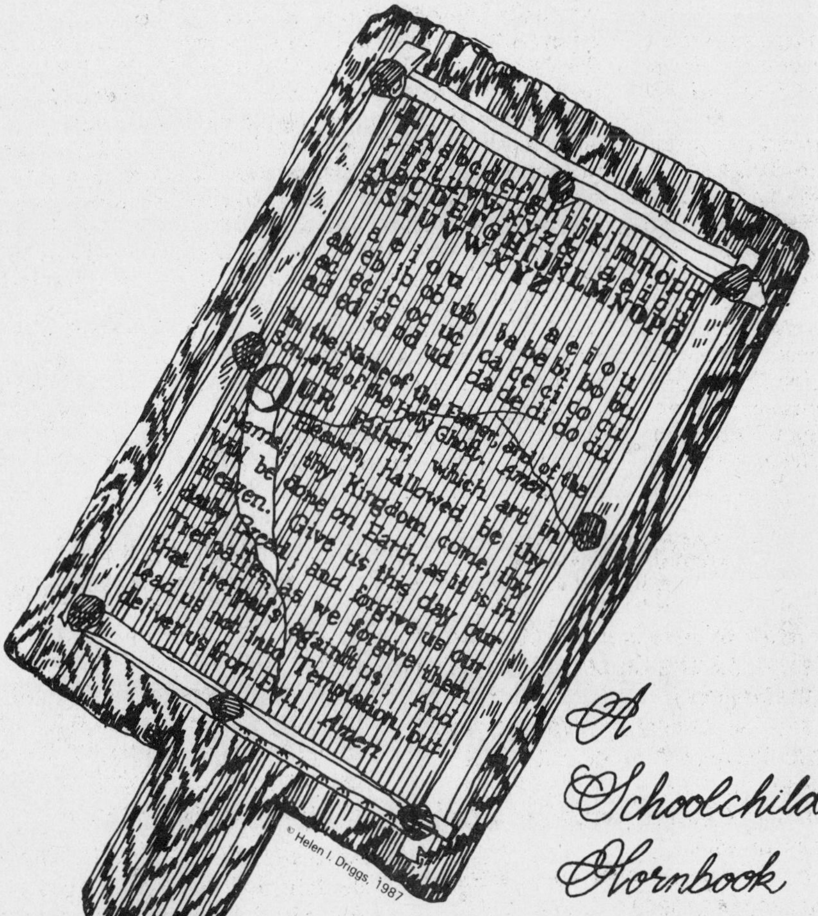

A Schoolchild's Hornbook

LIFESTYLE 1787

Todd House

Fourth and Walnut Streets. Open 9 a.m. to 5 p.m. daily. Tickets are required for admission; they may be obtained for free at the Visitor Center, Third and Chestnut Streets. 597-8974.

A young Quaker couple, John Todd and Dolley Payne Todd, bought this three-story brick house on the corner of Fourth and Walnut Streets in 1791. Compared with their neighbors down the block (Bishop White's family), the Todds lived very simply.

Like most people at the time, John Todd conducted business from home. There were no office buildings or factories for most people to go to. The front room in houses was often the shop or office. John Todd was a lawyer, and the spot that is a parlor in the Bishop White House is a law office in the Todd house, with desks for the lawyer and his clerk.

The other downstairs rooms are a sort of dining room-living room combination and, in the back, a kitchen. Upstairs, the front room is a parlor. Notice the plain white English creamware tea set, as compared with Bishop White's china. There are both a teapot and a coffeepot on a tea tray. Coffee was a growing custom in the country. Remember the Boston Tea Party. How might coffee have been a sign of the new America?

Across the hall is the couple's bedroom, and behind it is a maid's room. Even a young family of the middle class was likely to have a servant or two, and the servants usually lived in the house. In the Todds' house, the staff included Todd's law clerk, who slept up on the third floor.

Dolley's maid, at least for a while, was her 12-year-old sister, whose room conveniently has stairs down to the kitchen. As a younger girl, she might have used a "hornbook" to learn lessons. It was piece of parchment with the alphabet, numbers and perhaps some Bible verses, attached to a board. A very thin plate of animal's horn was secured over it so that it wouldn't tear. Real books were much too expensive for most people.

The Todds' two infant sons would probably have slept in their parents' bedroom, where you can see a chamber pot and a bed warmer, two items of nighttime comfort.

The yellow fever epidemic of 1793 killed John Todd, his mother and father, and one of the Todd children, as well as many of their friends. The house that Dolley and John occupied with their two children for such a short time gives us a good look at the simple yet comfortable life of a young, middle-class couple.

ON THE SPOT

Among many items that tell the story of life at the time, can you find:

The miniature tea set? It was not a doll's set, but was used to teach Dolley's sister how to serve tea properly.

The Philadelphia pretzelback settee in the parlor? Why was it called that? How does it compare with the sofa in Bishop White's parlor?

The market baskets in the kitchen? Without refrigerators, a trip to the market was a daily necessity.

The saltbox over the fireplace? Why was it kept there?

The irons on the mantel? How do you think they worked?

The cutting bowl and the mortar and pestle? These were the food processor and blender of their time.

The mousetrap? Do you think we have built a better one?

☛*Answers: The tea set is in the back bedroom.*

The pretzelback sofa's back does really look like a pretzel — two Philadelphia traditions meet! It is a much more modest piece of furniture than Bishop White's.

The baskets are the ones with the stout arm handles.

The saltbox over the fireplace stored salt, which of course didn't come in cardboard containers in those days. Heat from the fire helped keep it from getting lumpy in damp weather.

The irons aren't electric, of course. They are flatirons and were set on the coals in the fireplace to get hot. You'd need several, so you could keep ironing as each one cooled down.

The cutting bowl and mortar and pestle are on the table under the window.

The mousetrap is the heavy wooden box in the corner. It looks pretty deadly, doesn't it?

PRIVATE LIVES

The Todd House, where the young Dolley Todd lived with her first husband, John Todd, is a stone's throw from Independence Hall, where Dolley's future husband, James Madison, spent the summer of 1787 at the center of the constitutional debates.

It is tempting to wonder whether they met that summer. The answer is almost certainly no. First of all, the Todds didn't live in the house until 1791. In the summer of 1787, James Madison was pining for a fiancee whom he thought had jilted him, a Miss Polly Floyd of Long Island. (Miss Floyd was only 15. Although Madison had thought he was engaged to her, she and her family had other ideas.)

History reports that Madison and Mrs. Todd, by then a widow, were first introduced in 1794 — by Aaron Burr.

Dolley Todd did, of course, become Dolley Madison. She was a popular first lady, known for her quiet charm and intelligence, during Madison's presidency, 1809 to 1817.

LIFESTYLE 1787

LIFESTYLE 1787

Bishop White House

309 Walnut St. Open 9 a.m. to 5 p.m. Daily. Tickets are required for admission; they may be obtained for free at the Visitor Center, Third and Chestnut Streets. 597-8974.

William White was the minister of Christ Church in Philadelphia and the bishop of the Episcopal Church in Pennsylvania. In 1787 he was 39 years old and already an important man because of his position in the church and his reputation as a patriot.

White had been chaplain of the Continental Congress during the Revolution and later was chaplain of the U.S. Senate. His family also was fairly wealthy, and in the Bishop White House you can clearly see how the upper class lived in the cities of 1787.

In the front parlor you see the room where guests were received formally for tea. The bishop had five children and 11 grandchildren, who might have played in the "children's corner" of this room while the grownups talked.

Bishop White had all kinds of visitors because of his position — the benches in the front hall were where they waited to see him. If the visitor was a friend, he might be escorted to the back of the dining room, where the bishop liked to sit informally over a glass of wine or perhaps a cup of hot punch and smoke a clay pipe.

Delegates to the convention might very well have sat here and talked about old times or current events with Bishop White, who had been a friend and adviser over the years.

For private discussions, a visitor might go upstairs to the bishop's study. A painting of the study was made right after the bishop's death in 1836, so we know exactly how it looked. The painting is actually in the study, so you can see how faithfully the room has been restored — most of the objects in it were once actually used by Bishop White.

Unlike Benjamin Franklin's descendants, who didn't pay attention to preserving their famous forebear's home or belongings, Bishop White's descendants kept much of his personal property.

Next door to his study is the bishop's bedroom. You can see the net curtains around the bed. Window screens had not been thought of in 1787.

The bishop's house was near a livery stable and a tannery, where animal hides were processed into leather. Both places attracted a lot of flies, and the net curtains on the beds of the time helped sleepers ignore the flies and mosquitoes. Ignoring the smells and noise from the tannery and stables might not have been so easy on a muggy Philadelphia night.

In the bedroom you also see the bishop's washstand, which took the place of a bathroom sink in an era of no indoor bathrooms. On the bed are the bishop's lap desk and writing equipment — he often worked on sermons and letters late at night or early in the morning.

Upstairs is the third floor, which eventually became a sort of dormitory for a number of his orphaned grandchildren.

At the rear of the first floor, the indoor kitchen gives us a rich idea of the life of the time. The huge fireplace with its swarms of kitchen tools so different from our own served as a stove, oven and heater.

An indoor kitchen was common in fancy city houses. Poorer families might have no kitchen. In the country, the kitchen was often a separate building.

But Bishop White's family didn't stop at one kitchen fireplace. In the cellars below the kitchen were additional fireplaces and ovens for the large amounts of food the family and its guests would need. The underground rooms also included places to store food and a wine cellar. Barrels of wine were delivered through a trapdoor at the front of the house.

Behind the kitchen is an indoor toilet, a truly rare feature in those days. Called the "necessary," it has a seat that was designed for the grandchildren.

The bishop's family clearly enjoyed being up to the minute. Besides the convenience of the "necessary," they had clothes closets — another new idea, but only for the wealthy; remember, most people had only one or two sets of clothes.

The Whites also had the latest thing in dinnerware — blue-and-white china imported from the Orient, which had opened to American trading ships only the year before.

You can see the china, which actually belonged to the White family, in the dining room and the kitchen pantry.

ON THE SPOT

Can you find:

The kitchen pot called a "spider"? Why was it named that? Why was it designed that way?

Look in the kitchen for 1787's toaster and popcorn popper. How do they compare with what we have today?

When the woodwork in the bishop's study was scraped to remove layers of paint, a number of burn marks were found on a ledge by the fireplace. A close look at the painting of the study shows cigar butts on that ledge! Can you find them?

☛*Answers: The spiders are the pots with the legs. With legs, they could sit right in the coals of the fire, the hottest part, without getting ashes in the food.*

The toaster is the strange-looking flat device with the long handle in or near the fireplace. No pop-up toast here!

Cigar butts like those in the painting have been placed on the ledge by the fireplace.

18th-century Gardens

A colonial garden contributed more than food. Herbs were grown for medicines and creams, for food seasonings, and for dyes for yarn and cloth. Perfumes, blended from flowers, were added by housewives to soap and cosmetics.

Teas, wines and brandies, and jams and jellies were produced from fruits and berries. The colonists stopped drinking tea shipped from England after the British added high taxes to the price. Instead, the colonists drank their homemade teas.

The kinds of trees, bushes, flowers, vegetables and herbs in Independence Park today are the same kinds people grew in the colonies at the time of the Constitutional Convention.

Behind the **Todd House** at Fourth and Walnut is a garden that in the 1700s might have contained almost any of the vegetables and herbs we use today: beans, peas, squash, lettuce, beets and spinach fresh in summer; carrots, turnips, potatoes, onions and cabbage stored in the root cellar for winter. Herbs would include mint, thyme, sage, savory, parsley, marjoram and many others.

Next to the **Bishop White House** at Third and Walnut Streets is a more formal garden, with patterns made by hollies and boxwood.

The **Pennsylvania Horticultural Society** (625-8250) also maintains a formal garden on Walnut Street between Third and Fourth with an orchard and a little open house in which to sit and rest. It's free and open 9 a.m. to 5 p.m. on weekdays and 9 a.m. to dusk on weekends.

Popular flowers in 1787 would have included tulips, daffodils, crocuses and lilacs in the spring; poppies, snapdragons, begonias, foxglove, roses, lilies, pinks and carnations in the summer, and asters in the fall. Apple, peach, plum, pear and cherry were popular trees for the orchard.

The Philadelphia Society for Promoting Agriculture, the same society that George Washington and Samuel Powel would have attended, shares space with the Horticultural Society at 335 Walnut St. In 1787, farmers were very interested in what we now call conservation, and the society gave prizes for good use of land.

Elfreth's Alley

Between Front and Second Streets, Arch and Race Streets.

Every day for more than 250 years, people have been living along Elfreth's Alley. No other street in the United States can boast as much. The street, which was opened in 1701, came to be named after the Elfreths, a family of craftsmen who owned land in the neighborhood.

Middle-class craftspeople like the Elfreths lived and worked in these brick rowhouse trinities. They made household goods to order and to sell at market. Members of the Constitutional Convention might have bought these people's wares. A free museum, which displays some of them, is at 126 Elfreth's Alley. It's open 10 a.m. to 4 p.m. daily.

ON THE SPOT

Can you find Philadelphia "busybodies" hanging outside on the second-floor front walls? What were they used for?

☛*Answer: The busybodies are the little mirrors that enable people, without revealing that they are home, to see who's at the door — a handy invention for maintaining privacy.*

Outside the City of 1787

Visiting was a great source of entertainment in 1787, and the delegates did their share of it. Some of them certainly spent days off with friends who were fortunate to have homes in the country. The country, at that time, began somewhere not too far west of Seventh Street. By the time you got to the banks of the Schuylkill, you were really far from town.

In Fairmount Park, we can visit homes that actually were the country estates of the time. We know that Ben Franklin was a visitor at **Woodford**, where you can see a wind harp on the sill of the bedroom window. Look for the book closet with the lock on it (books were expensive), and the scalp scratcher. Can you think what it was for?

Other "country homes" in Fairmount Park include **Laurel Hill, Strawberry Mansion, Cedar Grove** and **Lemon Hill.**

LIFESTYLE 1787

Outside the Historic Mile: 'North of Market' and Society Hill

People who lived in 1787 naturally didn't think of themselves as living within a historic district. That's our way of looking at the oldest part of Philadelphia. As the city grew, some areas were more fashionable than others. Neighborhoods had begun.

Society Hill was a name that had nothing to do with high society. The land originally belonged to something called the Free Society of Traders, who got a lot of land from William Penn. Nevertheless, a number of wealthy and middle-class people did build homes there. Among them were Mayor Samuel Powel and wealthy merchant Henry Hill. The **Powel House** and the **Hill-Physick-Keith House** are two that may still be visited today.

In 1787, the area that was later called "North of Market" was a growing working-class neighborhood of modest but not poor homes. Betsy Ross lived there, and the street called Elfreth's Alley survives to tell us how the master craftsmen might have lived. These houses usually had a shop on the first floor and living quarters upstairs.

The less-fortunate day laborers might walk a mile or more into the city each day from areas we call Southwark or Queen Village (south of South Street) and Northern Liberties (north of Vine). Spring Garden Street was a farm area.

Along Market Street, down the middle of the street, were stalls where farmers, fishermen and craftsmen sold their goods three days a week. The farmers came in from New Jersey and the Pennsylvania countryside in wagons, slept on the wagons overnight to protect their goods from thieves, and set up their stalls in the early morning.

North of what is now Race Street and near the river was an area called Helltown, where the city's "low life" lived in shacks, caves or on the streets, ready to rob or swindle sailors on leave in the port of Philadelphia. The pickpockets and hustlers would roam the market, too, trying to take advantage of the farmers or their customers.

SOME THINGS TO WRITE ABOUT

Here are three writing projects that might be fun on a wet afternoon — or as assignments in school.

Write a news article about the Constitution, dated Sept. 17, 1787.

You visit Philadelphia between May and September 1787. Write a letter home to your best friend, who has never been here.

You are a delegate. Write a page for your diary or journal, describing a typical day. You may want to mention the frustration of not being able to tell anyone about what you're doing — even your family, whom you probably miss a lot by now.

(Some points to remember: What's good and what's bad about Philadelphia? The heat, the flies, the dirt, versus the market, concerts and plays, gardens, shipbuilding, the excitement of being in the Western world's biggest city.)

FIND THE SIGNERS

There were 55 delegates to the Constiutional Convention, and 39 of them signed the final document. Can you find the 39 signers of the Constitution?

Their names are hidden in these letters, horizontally and vertically, frontwards and backwards. There are no diagonal names. Try to circle all the names. You might want to use a pencil so the marks don't come through the paper onto the cutouts on the other side.

One signer is listed twice. Can you find him? (Look for the Z's.)

If the puzzle is a little too hard, you can find a hint that will help you by looking at the back page.

Here are the signers and the states they represented. The states are not mentioned in the puzzle.

X Y O J B F G H F N R R E D F E R V O N N I R E D O E F R E T H E D F G
B P I E R C E B U T L E R S P Q G O S M N T U V F L X P E T H M B R K J
F L Y O I I O P M H L P Q Y R N E H C M S E M A J V R B F C O G C E E G
X R S J J I R P H G L G O C P Y C J H E U V L B C U W X I L M V N H U I
B O O O R Q G Q U I U W M G M E S O A O T T S K O D R Y N S A D O W W G
L O W N K L E N H A S V A F R L H H R K B U P T P J E Q E D S N Q O Y D
L M N A U J R V I P R K H L F R I N L M O O R B B O C A J P F I T R R V
B O O T L K E I X S E E R U B A G L E C B I R N J A M E S W I L S O N P
B C S H U K A Y T D G E O R G E W A S H I N G T O N P E A S T K O G B O
W O V A D J D K S R N L G H T R S N C L L N Q O H O N O M N Z N I E Y Q
T H T N U O L B M A I L L I W B M G O M N O P I N M J K O M S A D R L R
T O O D B H B C J H O I E D E D L D T T E S S A B D R A H C I R F S G T
B R E A K X I H C C E X I T K I R O E B P P I G L K F L T E M F X H C E
U P Q Y V W G Y Y I R B N J S V Q N S G S R R T A U V E T P O N W E U C
H E L T V F D A B R A H A M B A L D W I N P R L I O Y X S Q N I N R M C
B O O O W E F G X U J I H D D D F O O F T P O K R X Q A F X S M Y M R W
L O O N Y B C E H W H X T Y F E E F K H G G M H I J J N O G F A K A L M
F U N N O S R E T A P M A I L L I W T H I J R U K W O D L W S J E N L M
L O S E O B D E F G F E N O I L E G H S J H U I V F H E E H I N E J B V
F U R S I R R O M T R E B O R D R O P P R Q E K J R N R I U N E D S T C
C A R E B C C D B H D Y W J O H N D I C K I N S O N R H N S O B C D Q B
T A K I N G C D R O F D E B G N I N N U G F R Y L K U A A J S B T J U R
B L O C K N Y B G M H C C S O G D L C K J Y E Q M M T M D P M N P O O N
D E E B R C L C H A R L E S P I N C K N E Y V N A M L I G S A L O H C I
F I D D L Y F K O S B L O V E F R I N G E S U C H N E L O L I G R S N K
S T O N R F R O M M L O P N C R F L E P S D O G H N D T G D L P F G J K
R O L L I N G X L I E R S T R R E M Y L C E G R O E G O O L L L J T M N
F I G G N I K S U F U R C R O W D E D H O U S E X L E N P C I R M N B D
S N O M I S Z T I F S A M O H T B R U C E S P R I N S T E E W N T O U G
V O L U M E F X R L O C R I M S O N L O X W I L L I A M J O H N S O N E
C R O C U S W I W I L L I A M L I V I N G S T O N B R U T E G N O M E P
M I D N I G H T R N W E F M A I L L I W M Y F O I R L O D Y U N T I E O
N O O N S P O O N L I I K S C R F L F O P D N M W Y B C L O H V L T M A
O R I G I N F O O T B N L L R E P J L D E C B S V I E Q P S E C D D P E
W O L F J J B Y C W N A O I S S P O K E R B E T S Y R O S S I N D P E D
W O W L J A M E S M A D I S O N J I M M Y D E C L R T I O N M C N R L O

- ☐ Abraham Baldwin, Ga.
- ☐ Richard Bassett, Del.
- ☐ Gunning Bedford, Del.
- ☐ John Blair, Va.
- ☐ William Blount, N.C.
- ☐ David Brearley, N.J.
- ☐ Jacob Broom, Del.
- ☐ Pierce Butler, S.C.
- ☐ Daniel Carroll, Md.
- ☐ George Clymer, Pa.
- ☐ Jonathan Dayton, N.J.
- ☐ John Dickinson, Del.
- ☐ William Few, Ga.
- ☐ Thomas FitzSimons, Pa.
- ☐ Benjamin Franklin, Pa.
- ☐ Nicholas Gilman, N.H.
- ☐ Nathaniel Gorham, Mass.
- ☐ Alexander Hamilton, N.Y.
- ☐ Jared Ingersoll, Pa.
- ☐ Daniel of St. Thomas Jenifer, Md.
- ☐ William Johnson, Conn.
- ☐ Rufus King, Mass.
- ☐ William Livingston, N.J.
- ☐ John Langdon, N.H.
- ☐ James Madison, Va.
- ☐ James McHenry, Md.
- ☐ Thomas Mifflin, Pa.
- ☐ Gouverneur Morris, Pa.
- ☐ Robert Morris, Pa.
- ☐ William Paterson, N.J.
- ☐ Charles Pinckney, S.C.
- ☐ Charles Cotesworth Pinckney, S.C.
- ☐ George Read, Del.
- ☐ John Rutledge, S.C.
- ☐ Roger Sherman, Conn.
- ☐ Richard Spaight, N.C.
- ☐ George Washington, Va.
- ☐ Hugh Williamson, N.C.
- ☐ James Wilson, Pa.

ANSWER ON PAGE 42

JUST FOR FUN

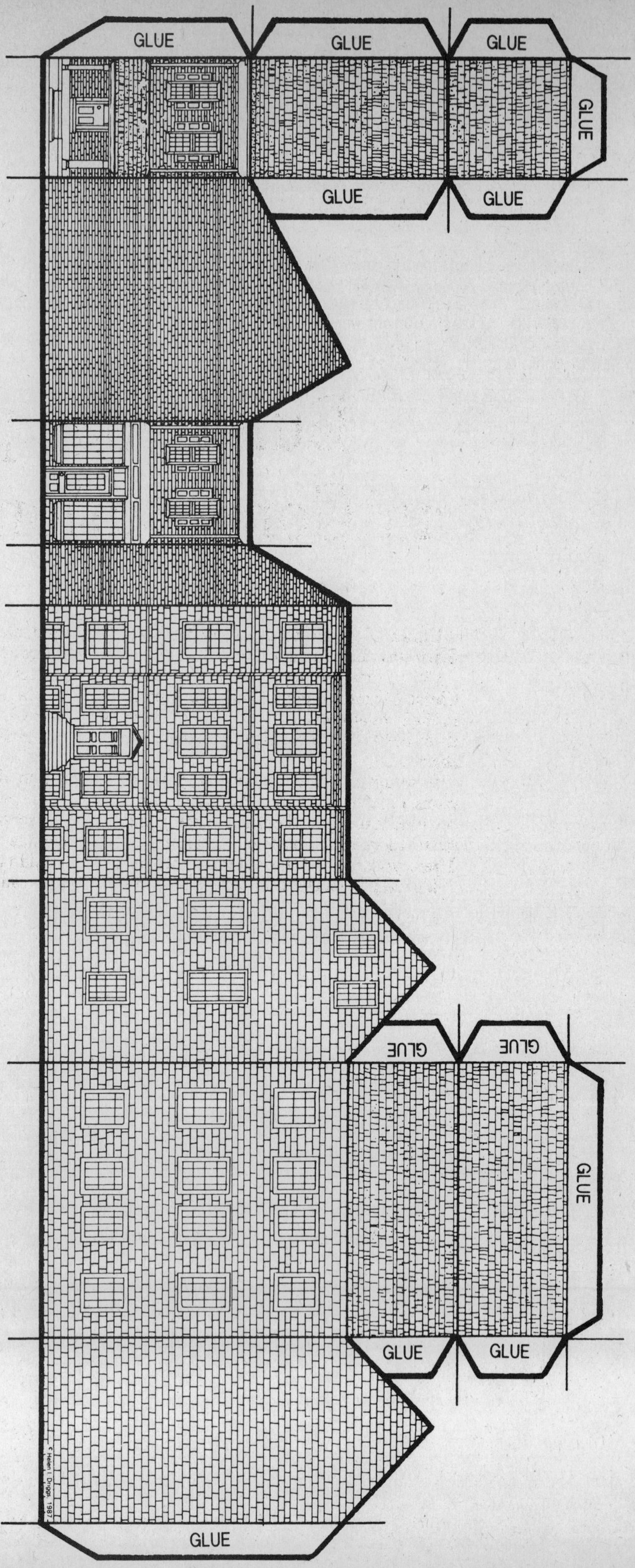

CITY TAVERN

1. Photocopy drawing on heavy card stock if desired.
2. Color with felt-tip pens, crayon or colored pencils.
3. Using a straightedge and Xacto knife, (or scissors if you are very young), cut out the drawing along the very heavy outlines. Be sure to clip the glue flaps free where the roof meets the side walls.
4. Fold along the lines of medium thickness. The side building extends forward, so be sure to fold in the right direction.
5. Glue where indicated, and attach glue flaps to the inside of the building.

Build your places in Constitution history

Here's a chance to use construction paper for construction.

City Tavern, Independence Hall and Christ Church all played important parts in the lives of the delegates in 1787. These three plans should enable anyone to build them.

It would be great to photocopy these plans onto heavy paper, but it is also possible just to cut them out roughly and paste them onto construction paper. Then, you can do the detailed cutting.

It's very important to slice along the solid black lines everywhere, not just where they form the outline of the project. Sometimes, you will need to make a slice to free one portion of a building from another, so that a fold can be made that will allow it to stand up.

Be careful, however, to stop when you get to the end of solid black line.

In real life, these buildings are all made of red brick, and the wood on their outside is generally painted white. But wouldn't they look snappy in deep purple and canary yellow?

JUST FOR FUN

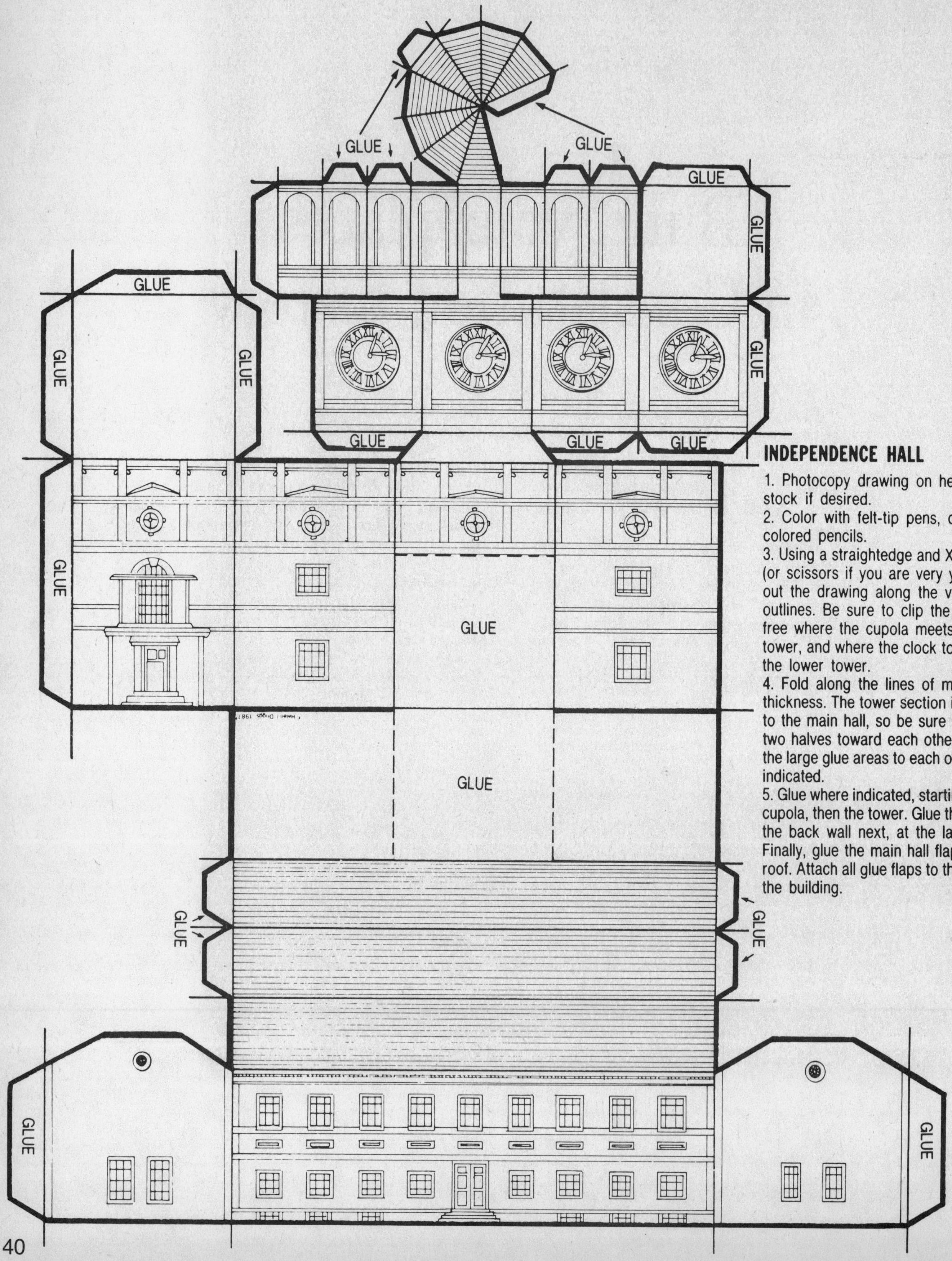

INDEPENDENCE HALL

1. Photocopy drawing on heavy card stock if desired.
2. Color with felt-tip pens, crayon or colored pencils.
3. Using a straightedge and Xacto knife, (or scissors if you are very young), cut out the drawing along the very heavy outlines. Be sure to clip the glue flaps free where the cupola meets the clock tower, and where the clock tower meets the lower tower.
4. Fold along the lines of medium thickness. The tower section is attached to the main hall, so be sure to fold the two halves toward each other to attach the large glue areas to each other where indicated.
5. Glue where indicated, starting with the cupola, then the tower. Glue the tower to the back wall next, at the large patch. Finally, glue the main hall flaps and the roof. Attach all glue flaps to the inside of the building.

JUST FOR FUN

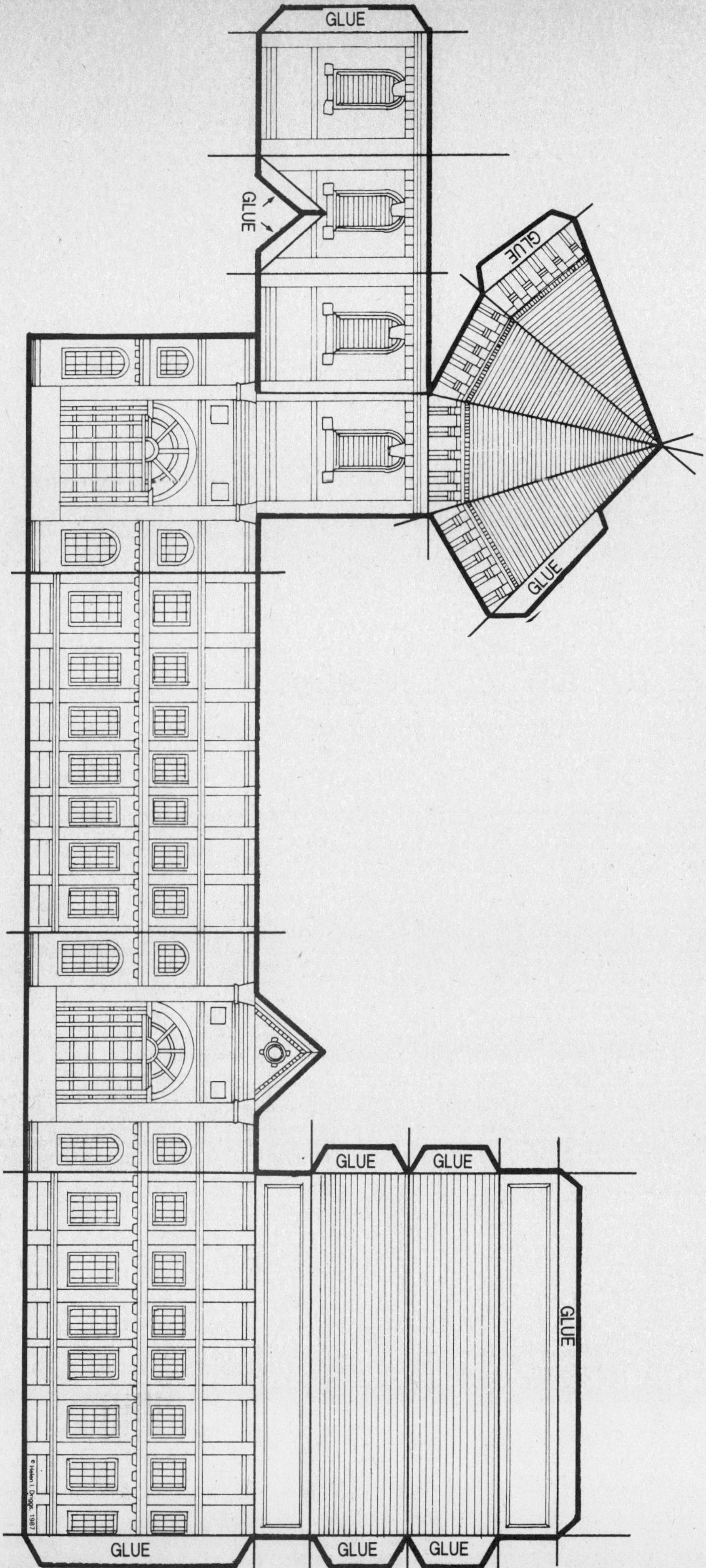

CHRIST CHURCH

1. Photocopy drawing on heavy card stock if desired.
2. Color with felt-tip pens, crayon or colored pencils.
3. Using a straightedge and Xacto knife, (or scissors if you are very young), cut out the drawing along the very heavy outlines. Be sure to clip the glue flaps free at the cut-out for the roof peak, and where the bell tower joins the font wall.
4. Fold along the lines of medium thickness.
5. Glue where indicated, starting with the bell tower. Be sure to glue the flaps connecting the tower to the roof. Attach all glue flaps to the inside of the building.

JUST FOR FUN

SOLUTION TO "FIND THE SIGNERS"

X Y O J B F G H F N R R E D F E R V O N N I R E D O E F R E T H E D F G E
B P I E R C E B U T L E R S P Q G O S M N T U V F L X P E T H M B R K J H
F L Y O I I O P M H L P Q Y R N E H C M S E M A J V R B F C O G C E E G U
X R S J J I R P H G L G O C P Y C J H E U V L B C U W X I L M V N H U I O
B O O O R Q G Q O I O W M G M E S O A O T T S K O D R Y N S A D O W W G S
L O W N K L E N H A S V A F R L H H R K B U P T P J E Q E D S N Q O Y D L
L M N A U J R V I P R K H L F R I N L M O O R B B O C A J P F I T R R V X
B O O T L K E I X S E E R U B A G L E C B I R N J A M E S W I L S O N P A
B C S H U K A Y T D G E O R G E W A S H I N G T O N P E A S T K O G B O S
W O V A D J D K S R N L G H T R S N C L L N Q O H O N O M N Z N I E Y Q C
T H T N U O L B M A I L L I W B M G O M N O P I N M J K O M S A D R L R X
T O O D B H B C J H O I E D E D L D T T E S S A B D R A H C I R F S G T H
B R E A K X I H C C E X I T K I R O E B P P I G L K F L T E M F X H C E D
U P Q Y V W G Y Y I R B N J S V Q N S G S R R T A U V E T P O N W E U C P
H E L T V F D A B R A H A M B A L D W I N P R L I O Y X S Q N I N R M C B
B O O O W E F G X U J I H D D D F O O F T P O K R X Q A F X S M Y M R W T
L O O N Y B C E H W H X T Y F E E F K H G G M H I J J N O G F A K A L M X
F U N N O S R E T A P M A I L L I W T H I J R U K W O D L W S J E N L M N
L O S E O B D E F G F E N O I L E G H S J H U I V F H E E H I N E J B V I
F U R S I R R O M T R E B O R D R O P P R Q E K J R N R I U N E D S T C D
C A R E B C C D B H D Y W J O H N D I C K I N S O N R H N S O B C D Q B K
T A K I N G C D R O F D E B G N I N N U G F R Y L K U A A J S B T J U R V
B L O C K N Y B G M H C C S O G D L C K J Y E Q M M T M D P M N P O O N C
D E E B R C L C H A R L E S P I N C K N E Y V N A M L I G S A L O H C I N
F I D D L Y F K O S B L O V E F R I N G E S U C H N E L O L I G R S N K M
S T O N R F R O M M L O P N C R F L E P S D O G H N D T G D L P F G J K L
R O L L I N G X L I E R S T R R E M Y L C E G R O E G O O L L L J T M N P
F I G G N I K S U F U R C R O W D E D H O U S E X L E N P C I R M N B D Y
S N O M I S Z T I F S A M O H T B R U C E S P R I N S T E E W N T O U G H
V O L U M E F X R L O C R I M S O N L O X W I L L I A M J O H N S O N E T
C R O C U S W I W I L L I A M L I V I N G S T O N B R U T E G N O M E P N
M I D N I G H T R N W E F M A I L L I W M Y F O I R L O D Y U N T I E O L
N O O N S P O O N L I I K S C R F L F O P D N M W Y B C L O H V L T M A L
O R I G I N F O O T B N L L R E P J L D E C B S V I E Q P S E C D D P E L
W O L F J J B Y C W N A O I S S P O K E R B E T S Y R O S S I N D P E D E
W O W L J A M E S M A D I S O N J I M M Y D E C L R T I O N M C N R L O P

CRYPTOGRAM

DV GSV KVLKOV LU GSV
FMRGVW HGZGVH, RM LIWVI
GL ULIN Z NLIV
KVIUVXG FMRLM, VHGZYORHS
QFHGRXV, RMHFIV WLNVHGRX
GIZMJFRORGB, KILERWV ULI
GSV XLNNLM WVUVMXV,
KILNLGV GSV TVMVIZO
DVOUZIV, ZMW HVXFIV GSV
YOVHHRMTH LU ORYVIGB
GL LFIHVOEVH ZMW
LFI KLHGVIRGB, WL LIWZRM
ZMW VHGZYORHS GSRH
XLMHGRGFGRLM ULI GSV
FMRGVW HGZGVH LU ZNVIRXZ

A "cryptogram" is a puzzle that involves code. Every letter in the puzzle stands for another letter. A "Z" may really be a "W." An "R" may really be an "A." In that case, every "Z" in the puzzle should stand for a "W," and every "R" should stand for an "A."

Most cryptograms are designed to be very hard, not using everyday words that can help give clues to the person solving the puzzle. This one, however, is not so hard. It's a famous quotation.

(Answers: Page 75)

Head
House
© Helen I. Driggs. 1987

Work for survival was a family affair, down on the farm

Although cities in America grew rapidly, most people in colonial days lived on farms, which provided everything a family needed — vegetables, grains, milk, meat, cloth and leather. Farmers in those days did not care so much about selling their produce. They mainly wanted to be sure to have enough to feed their own families.

The farmers around Philadelphia grew flax and raised sheep for wool. Their wives and daughters spun thread, dyed it and wove it into cloth. Then they cut the cloth and made dresses, trousers, shirts — whatever was necessary.

Men and boys cleared the land for farming. They fished and hunted deer, birds, rabbits and squirrels. They tapped the maple trees and boiled the sap to make syrup and maple sugar. Bees were kept for honey.

On the farm and in the city, boys were considered men at 16.

Farm women worked in their gardens during the growing season. They preserved food for eating the rest of the year. Butter and cheese were made by almost every housewife.

Vegetables, fruits and herbs were dried. Other vegetables and fruits, nuts, mushrooms and fish were pickled. Some food was stored in the dark, underground "cold cellar" or "root cellar."

Meat was smoked, made into sausage, or packed in salt or brine. Hides were tanned for leather. Grains were ground into flour or meal.

Some corn kernels were saved for popping. Corn husks were fashioned into ropes, mats and brooms or used as mattress stuffing. Corn cobs were used for the fire. Apples were dried, cooked for applesauce and apple butter, or pressed for cider. Everything was used.

There was no such thing as a wastebasket. If a family didn't need all it produced, the extra was sold at market.

Going to market

Your mother is busy with the new baby, so she asks you to go to market — to the new one, on Second Street, not the old one on High Street. She wants cornmeal, flour, eggs and milk. Too bad she won't give you money for candy.

You run up Third Street and over to Lombard. Out of breath, you walk slowly through the Head House shed at New Market, hoping to see Martha Washington or the mayor's wife. The butter-and-egg man says that Mrs. Washington has already come and gone and that Mrs. Powel sent one of her servants to do the shopping.

Two of your friends are with their mothers at the miller's stall. You agree to meet after lunch at the waterfront, to watch the ships unloading.

Your baby brother is asleep when you get back home. Mother thinks it's time you learn how to make cornbread, which early Americans called "journey cake" or "johnny cake."

Betsy Ross House

239 Arch St. Open 9 a.m. to 5 p.m. daily, Oct. 31 through April 30; 9 a.m. to 6 p.m. the rest of the year. Free. 627-5343.

Betsy Ross is best-known, according to legend, for sewing the first American flag, under the direction of George Washington. This story may or may not be true. Nobody knows for sure.

Two of Betsy's husbands were killed in the War for Independence. She and her third husband are now buried in the park in front of this house. Betsy had seven children, all daughters.

Although Quakers don't believe in fighting wars, Betsy Ross was one of the "fighting Quakers" of the Revolution. She made bullets for the Army's guns. To earn a living, she upholstered furniture and took in sewing.

In Betsy Ross' day, most city people lived and worked in small houses such as this one. No one knows for sure exactly which house was Betsy's, but it was in this neighborhood, and this house has been restored to represent her home.

ON THE SPOT

Can you find the bed warmer in the children's room? Why was it necessary?

☛*Answer: Fuel wouldn't be wasted to make a fire in a room where no one was going to be for most of the day. So the bedrooms could be cold at night. Bed warmers helped.*

RECIPE FOR JOHNNY CAKE

In a hot oven (425 degrees in a modern oven), place a greased eight-inch or nine-inch iron skillet. Now assemble your ingredients:

One egg
One cup buttermilk
Two tablespoons honey or maple syrup
Two-thirds cup cornmeal
Three-quarters cup flour (sifted, all-purpose)
One teaspoon baking soda
One teaspoon salt
Three tablespoons melted butter

Beat the eggs fluffy. Add the milk and sweetener.

Mix the dry ingredients and add gradually to the liquid. Add the melted butter and stir. Pour into the hot skillet and bake for 20 minutes or until light golden brown.

Powel House

244 S. Third St. Open 10 a.m. to 4 p.m. Tuesday through Saturday and 1 to 4 p.m. Sunday. During the summer, open 10 a.m to 5 p.m. Tuesday through Saturday and 1 to 5 p.m. Sunday. Admission: adults, $2; students, $1; children, 50 cents. 627-0364.

Imagine it! You're invited to a ball at the home of the mayor of Philadelphia. Maybe George Washington will be there.

A servant opens the door and welcomes you. You take a quick look around before going up the solid mahogany stairs. The mayor has the finest art collection in the United States, and you want to see some of it.

Samuel Powel and his wife, Elizabeth, greet you. The ballroom is magnificent. And the decorations in the supper room! Never have you seen such elegance. Everyone is celebrating Powel's return to office. He was mayor for a year before the Revolution. Now it's 1789, and he's mayor under the new Constitution.

You dance. You eat and drink. You talk. You hope to be invited again!

Visit the Powel House now, 200 years later, to see how the upper crust lived. There's the tea chest, so heavy it takes two people to lift it, and the Nanking china that George and Martha Washington presented to their good friends, the Powels.

Upstairs, the ballroom with its original ceiling and its splendid chandelier dominates. Mirrors reflected the gala balls held there, and musical instruments of the time may be seen here.

Mrs. Powel was considered one of the most brilliant hostesses of the day. John Adams wrote, almost groaning, after a dinner party there: "A most sinful feast again! Everything which could delight the eye or allure the taste: curds and creams, jellies, sweetmeats, twenty sorts of tarts . . . punch, wine, porter, beer, etc."

ON THE SPOT

Look for the "amity button" in the newel post — the upright post at the foot of the stairway — in the hall. The deed to the house was customarily stored here. Why?

☛*Answer: Probably because in case of fire, the front hall might be reached quickly.*

Hill-Physick-Keith House

321 S. Fourth St. Open 10 a.m. to 4 p.m. Tuesday through Saturday and 1 to 4 p.m. Sunday. Admission: adults, $2; students, $1; children under 12, 50 cents. 925-7866.

When this house was built in 1786, it was 20 feet wide and 100 feet deep. Over the years, rooms were added and the design was changed. Dr. Philip Syng Physick, who is called the father of American surgery, bought the 22-room house in 1790. Early in the 1900s, the neighborhood gradually became a slum. The house was neglected and rundown.

Happily, it was rescued and redone as it was in Dr. Physick's time. The house and furniture are in the Federal style, with 14-foot ceilings and, over the front door, the widest fanlight window in Philadelphia. The Argand lamps in the dining room are more than 200 years old.

The house is the only freestanding house of its period in Society Hill. It is the only Federal house in Philadelphia that has been restored with Federal-style furniture.

The gilt "George Washington" clock is one of nine known. In the drawing room is a blond mahogany couch made for Martha Washington's family. It indicates the skills of Philadelphia's furniture makers of that time.

ON THE SPOT

In an upstairs parlor, look for the inkstand that has Ben Franklin's name scratched on the back. Can you identify his thumbprints in the silver?

Bartram's House and Garden

54th Street and Lindbergh Boulevard. Gardens open dawn to dusk, daily. House open 10 a.m. to 4 p.m. Tuesday through Friday, through the end of April; 10 a.m. to 4 p.m. Tuesday through Sunday, May 1 through Oct. 31. Admission: adults, $2; children, $1. 729-5281.

John Bartram was America's first botanist, and his 300-acre farm is our first botanical garden. He studied plants of all kinds. One of his many achievements was to show colonial farmers how they could get 30 bushels of wheat per acre, instead of the usual 10.

His knowledge earned him a world reputation in his day; he was one of the Philadelphians, along with Franklin, whom foreigners most wanted to meet.

Only 27 acres of the farm remains. You can walk through the grounds, wander through Bartram's 18th-century house, wonder at the stone cider press down by the Schuylkill and admire the view.

ON THE SPOT

Bartram carved his religious philosophy in stone and included it in a wall of his house. Can you find it?

☛*Answer: It's on a windowsill, and it says:*
God alone
Almyty Lord
The Holy One
By me ador'd
— John Bartram 1787

OUR PAST ON DISPLAY

Betsy Ross' Victory Ball Shoe

Everywhere you look, the stuff of life, 1700s-style

All over Philadelphia are museums that offer permanent and special exhibits about lifestyles and events of the 1700s. Group tours are often welcome but should be arranged in advance.

Second Bank of the United States

420 Chestnut St. Open 9 a.m. to 5 p.m. daily. Tickets are required for admission; they may be obtained for free at the Visitor Center, Third and Chestnut Streets. 597-8974.

The Second Bank building, on Chestnut Street between the Visitor Center and Independence Hall, is no longer a bank. Now part of Independence National Historical Park, it is a museum that offers changing exhibits that relate to the area's history.

During this year's bicentennial celebration, the exhibit in the Second Bank of the United States shows *how* the "Miracle at Philadelphia" came to be.

The exhibit brings the documents, from the Declaration of Independence through the Constitution and beyond, to life. You can read Abigail Adams' discouragement in her letters from England: Will the United States ever be accepted as a country? You can get acquainted with the delegates and try your hand at making the choices they faced. Sign the Constitution yourself, and then go see how the ratification fight is going to be fought.

Army-Navy Museum at Pemberton House

Chestnut Street at Carpenters' Court, between Third and Fourth Streets. Open 9 a.m. to 5 p.m. daily. Free. 597-8974.

How did the United States Army and Navy develop in the 18th century? You can find out in Pemberton House. Inspect regiments in their uniforms. See a movie of the military at the time of the War for Independence. Watch the Battles of Saratoga and Lexington-Concord. Learn about the Revolution's greatest sea hero.

One of the problems the Constitutional Convention faced was how to continue and maintain the military force that defeated England. Pay for a private in the Army in 1776 had been 52 cents a *month!* And many had yet to be paid, even at that price, when the Constitution was being written.

At the Army-Navy Museum, you can stand on the slanting gun deck of a warship, cannonballs at your feet. At the hands-on exhibit, try to guide your ship in a sea battle when the wind is coming from the south.

The U.S. Marine Corps Memorial Museum

Carpenters' Court. Open 9 a.m. to 5 p.m. daily. Free. 597-8974.

The Marine Corps was founded in Philadelphia in 1775 at Tun Tavern, on the waterfront north of Dock Street.

The exhibits at this museum show the Marines in action during the Revolutionary period.

In 1787, New Hall was leased by the Army from the Carpenters' Company. The Army used the building for storage and a sort of repair shop before it was eventually torn down. The building that stands today is a reconstruction, designed to look just like the original. It was built in 1964-65.

"Rules for the Regulation of the Navy of the United States, 1776."

Rations/Saturday
1 lb. bread
1 lb. pork
½ lb. peas
4 oz. cheese
½ pt. rum
That's breakfast, lunch, dinner and snacks!

PATHWAY TO THE CONSTITUTION

D. Massachusetts is the only choice that will get you to the convention in Philadelphia. Ohio did not become a state until 1803. Vermont remained a separate country until it gained statehood in 1791. Rhode Island refused to send delegates.

2. May 30, 1787: Now the convention has begun, but what will the country be? Weak federation of strong states, or strong national government over the states? Gouverneur Morris of Pennsylvania says, "When the powers of the national government clash with the states, only then must the states yield." You think:

a. The states will lose all their rights if the central government gets any stronger.

b. A state should have the right to leave the union, or secede, if it wants to.

c. The country will not survive unless the states give up some powers.

d. State boundaries should be dissolved and the national government rule everything.

(What did the Constitution Framers decide? Go to Page 22.)

PONDER THIS

Think of ways in which the lives of wealthy people differed from the lives of others at the time of the Constitutional Convention.

OUR PAST ON DISPLAY

Atwater Kent Museum

15 S. Seventh St. Open 9:30 a.m. to 4:45 p.m. Tuesday through Saturday. Free. 686-3630.

Philadelphia grew from 2,200 people in 1700 to 81,000 a hundred years later. At the time of the Constitutional Convention, a city directory was needed to locate people and services. How did this growth happen? Find out at the the Atwater Kent, the Museum of the History of Philadelphia. You'll see how people worked, studied and played in 1787.

To keep order, constables patrolled the streets by day and watchmen patrolled by night. Volunteers fought fires. Water came from pumps or shallow wells.

It was felt that women belonged in the home. There was little chance for a career besides servant, nurse or seamstress. But there was Rebecca Jones, a Quaker traveling preacher. Some of her belongings are displayed here.

There was no such thing as free public education in those days. If they could afford it, parents paid to send their children to grammar school. Often churches ran schools and took in some children who couldn't pay. The Quakers had a school for children of free blacks; later, Quaker Anne Parrish started a school in her home to educate poor girls. The idea of taxing everyone to pay for free education was more than 30 years away.

There was no high school. Girls sometimes went to "finishing school." Boys often entered college at age 14. College students didn't have textbooks. They listened to lectures and made notes.

At the front of the museum building, two rooms show how volunteer services became paid city services. One contains pikes, axes and helmets used by early firefighters. It also has paintings, including one showing firefighters, rather than horses, pulling the engine along. In the same room is a police display, that includes two huge "mug books" of 19th-century criminals. In the other room, visitors can see how the city developed a safe and clean water supply.

The main exhibit area shows how people lived in Philadelphia, from the time of the Lenni Lenape Indians to 1900.

ON THE SPOT

At the Atwater Kent, look for Rebecca Jones' wraparound sunglasses; a lock of George Washington's hair (is it the color you expected?); a pocket watch, the kind that delegates to the Constitutional Convention would have carried; a spelling game from the time — the equivalent of colonial Scrabble, made of ivory; and the museum's Quaker dolls. One is black; the Quaker religion was open to all races.

Philadelphia Museum of Art

26th Street and the Benjamin Franklin Parkway. Open 10 a.m. to 5 p.m. Wednesday through Sunday. Open for guided tours 10 a.m. to 3 p.m. Tuesday. Admission: adults, $4; senior citizens, students and children under 18, $2. Free from 10 a.m. to 1 p.m. Sundays. 787-5431.

You could spend days at the Art Museum, one of the finest in the United States. Its steps are the ones that Rocky climbed to glory, but the true glory is inside, and all visitors to Philadelphia should make a stop here.

Of special constitutional interest is the American Wing, which holds works from some of the best early American furniture makers, silversmiths, clockmakers and painters, and works from later periods. This wing makes the point that American arts and crafts came from many cultures.

ON THE SPOT

Find Charles Willson Peale's *Staircase Group* painting in the American Wing. How does he fool the eye?

Peale knew everybody who was anybody during and after the Revolution, and he painted portraits of many of them. He organized America's first museum of natural history, and opened it to everyone —a new idea in those days.

He named his sons for long-dead famous artists — Raphael, Titian, Rembrandt, van Dyck and Rubens!

Philadelphia Maritime Museum

321 Chestnut St. Open 10 a.m. to 5 p.m. Monday through Saturday, and 1 to 5 p.m. Sunday. Admission by suggested contribution: adults, $1; children, free. 925-5439.

Nearly 900 ships were built in Philadelphia between the time that William Penn landed in 1682 and the Revolutionary War. But after the war, there was no navy. The colonies were still too disorganized to raise money and to agree on what was needed.

Merchants built ships for trade, however. European merchants were jealous of the Americans' success at trading and were delighted when pirates attacked and seized American ships and ransomed the crews. It was humiliating for the new country, which had no money to pay the ransoms.

Seven years after the Constitutional Convention, Congress finally ordered the construction of six frigates. One man-of-war, the 44-gun Philadelphia, was not only built in the city, but the money to build it was raised in Philadelphia, too. Now it was safe again to sail the seas.

At the Maritime Museum you can see the evolution of shipbuilding. Designs, blueprints, tools, models, furnishings, navigational instruments — they're all here. So, too, is a collection of 191 silver miniature ship models.

OUR PAST ON DISPLAY

Pennsylvania Hospital and Nursing Museum

Eighth Street and courtyard between Spruce and Pine Streets. The nursing museum and historic part of the hospital are open 9 a.m. to 4 p.m. Monday through Friday. Free. 829-3971.

Hospitals, 200 years ago, were not necessarily the place to go if you wanted the best health care. When people felt sick, they fetched the doctor, if they could afford to. If not, they tried to get to Pennsylvania Hospital on the outskirts of town.

It was the nation's first hospital, founded by — who else? — Benjamin Franklin and his friend Dr. Thomas Bond. They were concerned about the suffering they saw on Philadelphia streets. Building began in 1755.

In those days, there were no medical schools. Young doctors learned from older, more experienced ones. If they could afford to, they finished their studies in Europe.

At the time of the Constitutional Convention, Dr. Benjamin Rush was on the staff. He was a signer of the Declaration of Independence, a medical teacher, a social reformer and the "father of American psychiatry." His son was "insane." So was Charles Willson Peale's sister.

Until the late 1700s, the insane were chained up in basements, where curiosity-seekers could pay to see them. Dr. Rush, however, wanted to change all that, arguing that patients should get exercise and be given useful tasks to perform.

ON THE SPOT

When you visit the hospital, pick up a "script" on the second floor of the Pine Building, the original hospital on Pine, between Eighth and Ninth Streets. It will guide you through the building, where you can learn about 18th-century medical history.

Pennsylvania Academy of the Fine Arts

Broad and Cherry Streets. Open 10 a.m. to 5 p.m. Tuesday through Saturday (until 7 p.m. Wednesday), 11 a.m. to 5 p.m. Sunday. Admission: adults, $4; senior citizens and students, $2. Noon to 1 p.m. Tuesdays to Fridays, admission is $1. Free from 10 a.m. to 1 p.m. Saturdays. 972-7600.

Here is a museum that would be worth visiting even if it were empty. The building itself is astonishing, with decorations everywhere and a grand style.

The academy is the oldest fine arts school in the country, founded about 20 years after the Constitutional Convention. In 1876, it moved into the ornate Victorian building that is still its home. On exhibit is a fine selection of paintings by the artists who were best-known at the time: Charles Willson Peale, Benjamin West and Gilbert Stuart.

ON THE SPOT

Look for portraits of George Washington by Peale and Stuart, which are part of the Academy's permanent exhibit. While you're there, find West's huge, famous picture, *Penn's Treaty With the Indians*, painted nearly a hundred years after the event.

National Museum of American Jewish History

55 N. Fifth St. Open noon to 5 p.m. Sunday, 10 a.m. to 5 p.m. Monday through Thursday. Free until May 24; thereafter: adults, $1.75; students and senior citizens, $1.50; children, $1.25. 923-3811.

This museum has a section depicting life in the early years of the country. Included are a 1787 peddler's license signed by Ben Franklin, Torah bells from 1765, a Hanukah lamp of the same period and other items.

In 1789, when the Constitution was adopted and George Washington was inaugurated as the first president of the United States, a special Jewish "Prayer for the Country" was read in Richmond, Va.

Washington's letter of thanks to the Hebrew congregations of Philadelphia, New York, Charleston, S.C., and Richmond is at the museum to be read. It begins:

"Gentlemen: The liberality of sentiment towards each other, which marks every political and religious denomination of men in this country, stands unparalleled in the history of nations."

CONSTITUTION QUIZ 5

1. The Bill of Rights was ratified by all the states within two years after it was sent to them. True or false?
2. After the states approved the Constitution, what happened to the Continental Congress?
   a. It voted itself out of existence.
   b. It became the first new Constitutional Congress.
   c. The state legislatures dissolved it.
   d. The new president abolished it.
3. One requirement for being president is to be a "natural born citizen." What exactly does that mean?

(Answers: Page 75)

OUR PAST ON DISPLAY

How old this toy car from the Perelman Antique Toy Museum looks. It is a reproduction of one of the first big touring cars ever made, just a little after 1900. But for all its old-fashioned looks, it is still about 120 years newer than the Constitution. Imagine what people in the year 2107 will think of the cars we have today.

This car and many of the other illustrations in this guide make excellent pictures to color. Go right ahead and use pens, pencils or crayons on them.

OUR PAST ON DISPLAY

Perelman Antique Toy Museum

270 S. Second St. Open 9:30 a.m. to 5 p.m. daily. Admission: adults, $1.50; children, 75 cents. 922-1070.

Children made their own toys in the early colonial days — dolls, popguns, whistles, windmills, water wheels, toy weapons, tops and hobbyhorses. Children played after chores were done, but grownups didn't usually encourage children to play.

There weren't many toys sold in shops. The dolls that came from Europe were dressed in the latest fashions for Americans to copy and were very expensive.

As the United States grew, as made-by-machine took over made-by-hand, there were more and more toys and more and more people with money to buy them.

You can see more than 4,000 toys in the Perelman Antique Toy Museum.

Historical Society of Pennsylvania

1300 Locust St. Open 9 a.m. to 5 p.m. Tuesday through Friday, and 10 a.m. to 3 p.m. Saturday. Free. 732-6200.

The Historical Society is a treasure trove. Rare books on Pennsylvania history; newspapers — 1,600 of them — going back to the first one in Pennsylvania from 1719; the largest privately supported archives in the United States, a museum. It's all at the Historical Society.

The free galleries always exhibit treasures from the collection, organized around a theme. In the society's possession are Benjamin Franklin's music stand and a number of things — silver and china, a strong box and furniture — belonging to Robert Morris and William Penn's family.

In addition, the society has a free "History Hotline" that you can call to get a constitutional message. The number is 800-3B-PROUD. You can dial any time, through November.

Shoe Museum at the Pennsylvania College of Podiatric Medicine

Eighth and Race Streets. Open 9 a.m. to 5 p.m. Monday through Friday; call ahead, especially if arriving in a group. Free. 629-0300, Ext. 218.

The Shoe Museum exhibit, "Footwear Through the Ages," has shoes from all over the world, including some clogs from 1700s. The Egyptian burial sandals are thought to be more than 2,000 years old. Arnold Palmer's golf shoes were worn in 1983.

Among the many pairs, you can see shoes that belonged to the wives of several presidents.

Footwear was handmade until the late 1700s, when the first shoe factories were built in Europe. Authorities at the museum say there were no machine-operated shoe factories in the United States until the early 1900s!

Mutter Museum at the College of Physicians

19 S. 22d St. Open 10 a.m. to 4 p.m. Tuesday through Friday. Free. 561-6059.

The College of Physicians is a medical society, founded in 1787. It is celebrating its 200th birthday this year, too, and that's the constitutional reason for visiting here. The other reason is that it's *weird*.

The weird part is the Mutter Museum, with all sorts of displays of strange things that have to do with the study of medicine — skeletons with two heads, brains in jars. Here's where you can find the "Soap Lady." It's a mummy of a woman who is supposed to have died of yellow fever in 1792.

Less scary are displays that show what sorts of medicines doctors used around 1787. There's even a fur muff that a surgeon during the Revolutionary War used at Valley Forge. He had to keep his hands warm enough to operate on Gen. Washington's wounded soldiers.

Please Touch Museum

210 N. 21st St. Open 10 a.m. to 4:30 p.m. Tuesday through Saturday, and 12:30 p.m. to 4:30 p.m. Sunday. Admission: $3.50. 963-0667.

Here is a museum that's supposed to be especially for children (but just look around and see who's having the best fun). It has all sorts of exhibits that let visitors *do* things: dress up like anyone they want to be (such as a person from colonial days), play a calliope and other percussion instruments, pet animals — even perform in a circus.

PONDER THIS

Why was it important that the colonists should read about the new Constitution?

☛Answer: There was no radio or television. News traveled very slowly. The people were to be involved in ratifying, and they had to be persuaded. After the convention, men like Alexander Hamilton hurried home to begin a series of articles arguing in favor. Many argued against. The only way to make your point to the public was on paper.

National Archives of the United States, Philadelphia Branch

Ninth and Market Streets. Open 8 a.m. to 5 p.m. Monday through Friday and 9 a.m. to 1 p.m. the first and third Saturdays of each month. Free. 597-3000.

The National Archives keeps all the valuable records of the U.S. government. There are *billions* of items in the archives, in Washington and at branches in other cities, most of them available for research. There are always some interesting exhibits at the Philadelphia branch of the archives.

The first census in the country was taken in 1790. With independence won and a Constitution signed, we were a country to be reckoned with — and counted. In 1790, records tell us, there were five categories to be counted: "white males over 16, white males under 16, white females, other free persons and slaves." The job was accomplished by sending officials called marshals around to each house on foot.

ON THE SPOT

Pick up the free booklets that explain how you can find out about your ancestors by using census records, naturalization records, ship passenger lists and records of the Army, Navy, Marines and Coast Guard. The records go back to 1775!

OUR PAST ON DISPLAY

U.S. Mint

Fifth and Arch Streets. Open 9 a.m. to 4:30 p.m. Monday through Saturday. Free. 597-7350.

The first time "United States of America" was used on a coin was in 1787. The motto on the coin: "Mind Your Business."

In 1792, Philadelphia opened the first American mint. Metal was scarce. Citizens were asked to donate whatever they could. President Washington gave a copper teakettle and two pairs of tongs.

Some other donations include old nails, spokes, and parts from wrecked ships. If you had a job at the first mint, you worked from 5 a.m. to 8 p.m.

Here's the budget of the first U.S. Mint. No wages for employees are included.

Property purchase	$4,266.67
Straw, hay & horse medicine	2.00
Director's salary	2,000.00
Watch dog	3.00
Yard alarm bell	17.82
120 bushels of coal	38.00
6 lbs. old copper	1.00

The watchdog's name was Nero, and he was *mean.*

PATHWAY TO THE CONSTITUTION

A. Various lengths of time were kicked about: no requirements, five years, four years, then seven and nine. Delegates probably worried about "foreign influences": Let someone live here long enough so we're sure he's not a spy or an agent of some foreign country.

9. Aug. 30, 1787. Who will ratify this Constitution?

a. All 13 states, of course. Under the old Articles of Confederation, any changes must be agreed to by all.

b. James Wilson suggests that the Constitution will be ratified when seven states approve it. That's a majority. You agree.

c. You argue that the people, not the states, must have the power to ratify. After all, that's what this is all about. A majority of people throughout the states should approve the document.

d. You think that the people should vote, but that the decision should come through the states. Unanimous approval sounds unreasonable, but it's such a big step that more than a simple majority should be required.

(What did the Constitution Framers decide? Go to Page 30.)

SPECIAL EXHIBITS

To celebrate the 200th anniversary of the signing of the Constitution, many Philadelphia museums are offering special long-term exhibits. Here are some of them:

"Miracle at Philadelphia."
Second Bank of the United States
An excellent exhibit showing how the Constitution came to be. Through 1987.

"A More Perfect Union."
Historical Society of Pennsylvania
Pictures, letters and diaries of the delegates, and drafts of the Constitution. Maps and newspapers. June 18-Dec. 14.

"Federal Philadelphia 1785-1825: The Athens of the Western World."
Philadelphia Museum of Art
Silver, costumes, paintings, architecture of the period. July 5-Sept. 20.

"Framing the Constitution: The Artists' Record."
Pennsylvania Academy of the Fine Arts
Works on loan and from the permanent collection. Paintings and sculpture of delegates and Philadelphian movers and shakers. Through Dec. 13.

" 'Tis Done! We Have Become a Nation."
National Archives, Philadelphia Branch
Posters and a Pennsylvania copy of the Constitution. Mid-April through November.

"Red, White and Blue: Childhood and Citizenship."
Please Touch Museum
A hands-on exhibit that shows what it means to be an American child and what it meant in times past. June 2 through May 1988.

"A Promise of Permanency."
Independence Park Visitor Center
A hands-on computer exhibit that shows how to use the Constitution today. May 13 through 1992.

"Magna Carta."
Old City Hall
One of the original copies of the British document, signed in 1215, that was one of the forerunners of the Constitution. May through Dec. 31.

A Place to Worship

The 'Holy Experiment' that lasted

If you were a child in Philadelphia in 1787, you might have been born in the city, but chances are your parents or grandparents weren't.

They might have come to William Penn's city from England or from elsewhere in Europe. Their country probably had one official church, and those who didn't belong to it could end up in prison. In the Old World, people lost everything they owned and were even tortured or killed for refusing to join the official church. There was very little room for a difference in opinion or beliefs.

That was why William Penn came to the New World, to establish a city on the Delaware River. With him he brought an idea — the "Holy Experiment," as he called it.

Penn was born in England, a member of the nobility, and grew up in the official church of the kings of England. Then he became a member of the Religious Society of Friends, or Quakers, as they were called, and he went to jail for it.

But the king owed Penn's family money. To pay it off and get rid of a young troublemaker, he gave Penn a huge piece of land in the New World — Pennsylvania, meaning "Penn's Woods."

Here, Penn founded his city of brotherly love, Philadelphia, in 1683. "Force may subdue, but love gains," he said. "Let us then try what love may do." And so the Holy Experiment began, with the ideal of respecting the rights of every person.

By the time the delegates gathered in that summer of 1787 to write a Constitution for their country, Penn's "experiment" in religious freedom was more than 100 years old. It had seen some hard tests, it wasn't perfect, but it had survived.

People of all religions had heard of Penn and had come to Philadelphia, looking for freedom — first Quakers, then Protestants, Catholics and Jews. They found more freedom for everyone under the Holy Experiment than anyone had seen back home.

Some historians believe that the sense of freedom and tolerance for others in Philadelphia helped the writers of the Declaration of Independence and later the Constitution meet here safely, in peace.

The men who wrote these documents had strong and serious disagreements. Sometimes they fought bitterly, but they kept trying. In the end, enough of them agreed to sign the document we call the Constitution. They also promised to draw up a Bill of Rights to go with it, to protect certain freedoms for all citizens.

And so one freedom helped other freedoms grow. The Holy Experiment that William Penn started 100 years earlier provided the time and the place for the Constitutional Convention.

At the time of the Constitutional Convention, Philadelphia had a population of 40,000 to 50,000. There were Quakers, Anglicans, Catholics, Jews, Methodists, Presbyterians, Lutherans and more. Some groups had not one but several places of worship. Without exception, every group that came to the colonies started out meeting in people's homes until there was enough time and money to build a place to worship.

As a rule, the non-Anglican Protestant churches (such as Reformed, Methodist and Presbyterian) were rather plain. Catholic churches were more elaborately decorated. Anglican, or Episcopal, churches were somewhere in the middle. These differences can still be seen today in some of Philadelphia's churches. The Quaker meeting houses were the plainest of all, since the Friends made it a central rule to live simply.

An unusual feature of many of the older churches is that they do not have steeples. That was perhaps an example of the influence of Quaker simplicity on the city at large.

PATHWAY TO THE CONSTITUTION

C. It is decided that a two-thirds vote of Congress will override the president's veto.

5. June 9-11, 1787: The convention is deadlocked over how Congress will be elected. Will each state get the same number of representatives, or should representatives be allotted according to population?

a. You side with the big states. Let population determine how many representatives a state gets. Then the big states will be in power.

b. You are relieved when Roger Sherman of Connecticut suggests a "compromise": Let one house of Congress be chosen by population, and let the other have the same number of members from every state.

c. You side with the small states. All states will have the same number of representatives, so small states and big ones will be equal.

d. You believe that representatives should be elected "at large," and that state boundaries should not be considered.

(What did the Constitution Framers decide? Go to Page 15.)

A PLACE TO WORSHIP

A Place to Worship

You just woke up and — surprise! — you're back in 1787

It's Sunday, May 6, 1787. It's been spring for a month and more now, but it feels like winter in your room this morning as you struggle out from under the quilt that covers your cornhusk mattress. Everyone's saying it will be an unusually cool season if this keeps up. It's your turn to go downstairs and start the fire in the kitchen. You rake up coals from the night before and throw on firewood, which soon blazes up. The rest of the family hears you banging around and straggles down.

Father hears some Bible verses from each family member, and then you sit down to a breakfast of bread and milk — tea for grownups — on the wooden benches at the kitchen table.

You all had your weekly baths last night, taking turns in the copper tub by the kitchen fireplace. It was your sister's turn to haul the heavy buckets of water from the well, thank goodness. Then you all laid out your good clothes (dark dresses with a shawl and bonnet for the women and girls, knee breeches and vest for the men). You polished the family's shoes with a mixture of soot and linseed oil. Then you all sat in the kitchen again, while Father read from the Bible and led the family in prayers.

Breakfast is done and the prayers said. You quickly get into this year's suit of good clothes — a hand-me-down from one of your cousins, but still in pretty good shape. Your family isn't really wealthy — no carriage or horses. But your church is in your neighborhood — at least you don't have to pick your way across town, like some of your neighbors, through streets full of mud and garbage, getting splashed as the horses pass.

Church. You are sitting in your family's pew now, trying to follow the sermon. Religion is the center of the city's life in so many ways. Everyone who is anyone goes to church, or meeting or synagogue (if you were one of the very few Jewish people in Philadelphia in 1787, of course, you'd be worshipping on Saturday, not Sunday). Besides being for worship, those buildings are places where you meet your friends and get some of your education and often your news of the outside world. Grandmother often tells how her father was jailed for his religion — your family treasures its right to worship freely.

Still, the services are long, and the benches are hard. In some churches, services last all day, with just a little time out for midday dinner. You count yourself lucky that in your church you only have to go for three hours in the morning. In the afternoon you get to stay home.... Mother pokes you quietly in the ribs. She always seems to know when your mind is wandering. There's only a very little heat from a woodstove in the church, but at least there's the family footwarmer — sometimes no more than a bucket full of bricks that were heated in the fire before you left home, but it helps. In winter you bring blankets to church too, and the family huddles together in its box pew. The benches are hard. Sometimes you think that the good Lord, who knows everything, knows how hard they are, and how you sometimes just have to wiggle.... Another poke from Mother.

Then back home for Sunday dinner. No unnecessary work is allowed on the Sabbath, so Mother just heats up stew that was made yesterday with the bones of the chicken, some squirrels that Father shot, potatoes, dried beans, and dandelion greens from the kitchen garden. You spend a quiet afternoon, Father reading from the Bible while the women sew. You're allowed to play with a "Sunday toy" if you are good and quiet. Your favorite is the little Noah's Ark with its tiny toys, all painted two by two by your uncle, a cabinetmaker. The Sunday sitting room is dark, and the afternoon is long. Maybe someone will come to visit. Then the grownups are distracted, and sometimes the children even get sent outside to play ("But no noise and no running, mind!").

Supper is a little more stew with Mother's good bread. Then evening prayers by firelight, and off to bed. You fall asleep with a piece of great news buzzing in your head, news learned in church that day, but hardly discussed with the afternoon's Bible reading. The news: George Washington and the Virginians are coming to town next Sunday!

There's to be some kind of big meeting to try to straighten out all the arguments that states are having. Mother says it'll be like the great days of the Revolution all over again. But Father says it'll take more than a meeting to straighten out the country's money troubles. He says we need a miracle. And then Mother says, "Hush, not on the Lord's Day," and . . . you fall asleep.

A GLOSSARY

Some of the words used to talk about houses of worship may be unfamiliar. Here are a few of them, and their definitions:

Chalice — The cup used in church for the wine in Mass or Holy Communion. Often made of silver, it has a base and a stem.
Cherub — A kind of angel, usually painted as a child with rosy cheeks.
Congregation — A group of people who gather to worship.
Parish — A church district.
Rector — A minister or priest in charge of a parish.
Sexton — An employee who takes care of church property. He often rings the bells and digs graves.
Torah — The most important Jewish holy writings.

A PLACE TO WORSHIP

Then and now, step inside and find sanctuary

Christ Church

Second Street above Market. 922-1695.

Christ Church, built from 1727 to 1744, is not the oldest church still standing in Philadelphia (that's Gloria Dei), but it may be the one people think of when they think of the American Revolution and the years that followed. Its famous first rector, William White, was chaplain to the Continental Congress during the Revolution. He was a friend and adviser to some of the young nation's best-known leaders.

This Episcopal church in the heart of oldest Philadelphia looks much as it did in 1787, with an outside of brick, wooden box pews inside and the plain glass windows. The pews are called "box" pews because they are shaped like boxes (without tops, of course). Sometimes, they even have little doors.

A visitor who enters down the main central aisle can slip into Ben Franklin's pew (No. 70), with its plaque telling how he helped draft the Constitution. From there you can see the coat of arms hanging over George Washington's pew, No. 58, and the little American flag over Betsy Ross', No. 12.

Overhead is a large brass chandelier that held candles in Washington's time. Parishioners from 1787 would also recognize the carved wooden baptismal font, the silk-covered mahogany bishop's chair and the elegant gold and white "wine-glass" pulpit, built by a Philadelphia cabinetmaker in 1769. Why do you think they designed a pulpit that is shaped like a wine glass?

In the church's burial grounds lie four signers of the Constitution — Franklin, Robert Morris and James Wilson of Pennsylvania, and Pierce Butler of South Carolina.

We know the congregation of Christ Church enjoyed some comfort and even luxury in that time — one bill remains for 30 yards of silk lace for cushions in Washington's pew.

Arch Street Meeting House

304 Arch St. 627-2667.

The Religious Society of Friends began in England in the 1640s. Founder George Fox and others met to worship God in obedience to their own individual beliefs, or "inner light," and not in obedience to what any church said.

Fox told his hearers they should "tremble at the word of the Lord" — so people started calling the Friends "Quakers." The first Quaker settlers came to the banks of the Delaware in 1681, followed by William Penn a year later.

For about the first 80 years, Quakers were important in governing the city, but by 1787 most of them had withdrawn somewhat and put renewed emphasis on worship and faith.

The Quaker service, then as now, was framed in silence. Members would stand to speak if the spirit moved them, perhaps sharing some idea gathered from reading the Bible, perhaps relating it to daily life.

Men and women sat separately, and when the meeting had business to conduct, the men and women were actually separated by a screen or met in separate rooms. George Fox had suggested that the women's concerns would get a better hearing if they conducted their own meetings. Quaker women did have an independent spirit. They founded their own medical school, among other things. (It was Women's Medical College, which became Medical College of Pennsylvania.)

Quakers dressed plainly (the color gray is often mentioned in descriptions of their clothes), with round flat hats for the men and dark green or blue aprons for the women. Quakers were discouraged from dancing, singing or playing cards. They were forbidden to use alcohol or tobacco. They were sometimes "read out" of the meeting for marrying non-Quakers. Quakers disapproved of slave-owning.

The Arch Street Meeting House, built in 1804 between Third and Fourth Streets, is the largest in the world, but it otherwise looks much like the meeting house it replaced. It is a plain brick and wood building built in a "U" shape, with a small central meeting room and two wings.

Today the central room is used for weekly meetings, and the large west wing is used for yearly meetings of public functions. The east wing is a museum that traces the history of Penn's Holy Experiment and shows objects related to early Quaker life in the New World.

In the center room, some of the original benches may be seen, with the horsehair cushions that are even older than the meeting house. Visitors attending a meeting there will experience the same form and some of the same ideas that have served the Society of Friends in Philadelphia through three centuries.

Under the Arch Street Meeting House is the burial ground for an older meeting house that stood at Second and Market.

During the yellow fever epidemic that swept Philadelphia in the 1790s, people were buried in the Arch Street ground in mass graves. Some Quaker historians believe that at least 20,000 people are buried under the Arch Street meeting house, although more conservative estimates put the number at 4,000.

Benjamin Franklin arrived here in 1723 with only a Dutch dollar in his pocket. He had walked part of the way and taken boats the rest. He described his first day as a tired and hungry 17-year-old in Philadelphia:

"

I walked again up the street, which by this time had many clean-dressed people in it, who were all walking the same way. I joined them, and was thereby led into the great meeting-house of the Quakers near the market. I sat down among them, and, after looking around awhile and hearing nothing said, being very drowsy thro' labor and want of rest the proceding night, I fell fast asleep, and continu'd so till the meeting broke up, when one was kind enough to rouse me. This was, therefore, the first house I was in, or slept in, in Philadelphia.

"

PATHWAY TO THE CONSTITUTION

A. The idea of counting a slave as three-fifths of a person for government representation had been thought of in 1783. "All other persons," of course, meant slaves, a word that the Framers of the Constitution carefully avoided. The compromise pleased no one, but again, a compromise kept the process going.

7. Aug. 6, 1787, and following weeks: What to do about slavery? Tempers are flaring. Can the states be allowed to control it (meaning slavery will certainly continue in the South and spread to new territory in the West) or shall Congress control slavery, along with all other trade and commerce?

a. The South can't survive without slaves. You want state control.

b. You agree with Gouverneur Morris of Pennsylvania, who calls slavery a "curse." Even George Mason of Virginia says slavery is "infernal traffic." Only federal control can mean an end to this evil.

c. You disapprove of slavery, but you know the Southern states will pack up and go home if it's threatened. You compromise.

d. You believe the Constitution should go beyond just granting federal control and should specifically abolish slavery.

(What did the Constitution Framers decide? Go to Page 28.)

PONDER THIS

There was no electricity in those days. What kind of weather and what time of day were best for operations? Why were four strong men needed to hold down the patient?

☛Answer: Broad daylight and bright sun were best; operating "parlors" had big windows. There was no anesthetic in 1787. When a doctor cut, it hurt!

CONSTITUTION QUIZ 6

1. Northern delegates wanted slaves considered people, and Southern delegates wanted slaves considered property. True or false?

2. What is the most frequent subject of the 26 amendments to the Constitution?

3. At the time the Constitution was written, could most Americans vote?

4. Having come from immigrant families themselves, most delegates wanted to make it easy for immigrants to become citizens. True or false?

(Answers: Page 75)

A PLACE TO WORSHIP

Free Quaker
Meeting House

Free Quaker Meeting House

Fifth and Arch Streets. 923-6777.

The Quakers believed very strongly that war was bad. Most of them believed very strongly, too, that independence from England was good. In the 1770s, it became clear that the colonies would have to fight for independence. What were the Quakers to do?

Some stayed with their religious beliefs. About 200, however, became "fighting Quakers." They were banished from the regular Quaker meetings, so they built their own building.

It was the Free Quaker Meeting House, due north of Independence Hall at Fifth and Arch Streets, and they met there until 1834. Their numbers dwindled after the war, as they rejoined their old meetings. But the little meeting house remains and is open to the public as a small museum during the summer. In one exhibit case is a yellowed piece of paper cut into the shape of a star — the same piece, it is said, that Betsy Ross showed to George Washington when she was designing the first American flag.

Gloria Dei (Old Swedes') Church

916 S. Swanson St. (near Delaware Avenue and Christian Street). 389-1513.

The oldest church in Philadelphia (built in 1677) is also farthest from Center City, on a rise overlooking the Delaware at Christian Street. It has changed denominations, going from Lutheran to Episcopal in 1845, but it looks much as it did when its first members worshiped there, or when Betsy Ross married Capt. Joseph Ashbourn there in 1777.

The outside of the church is a fine example of the "Flemish bond" style of brick building that was also used for Holy Trinity Church, though they were built more than 100 years apart. The church still has and uses its original baptismal font. Also there since its founding are the gold sunbursts on the pulpit and lectern and the carved wooden cherub holding an open Bible with the painted quotation in Swedish: "Glory to God in the highest." (*Gloria Dei* means "the glory of God" in Latin.)

Hanging from the ceiling are models of the Swedish ships Fogel Grip and Kalmar Nickel that brought the first Swedes in 1638. There is also a carving of the angel Gabriel, as is common in churches in Sweden.

The Catholic Churches

Old St. Joseph's, 321 Willings Alley, near Fourth and Walnut Streets. 923-1733.

Old St. Mary's, 252 S. Fourth St., near Locust Street. 923-7930.

Holy Trinity, Sixth and Spruce Streets. 923-7930.

The history of the Catholic churches, especially St. Joseph's, is probably the most dramatic of the Philadelphia churches.

Under English law, public Catholic services were forbidden — even in the 13 colonies. A Jesuit priest, Father Joseph Greaton, settled in Philadelphia in the 1720s and built a handsome home near Fourth and Walnut. What neighbors didn't know was that the house was really a camouflage for a chapel.

The little chapel looked more like a kitchen than a church, they thought. But then Father Greaton went public in 1733, announcing St. Joseph's Church, the first open Roman Catholic church in America or England. Complaints went up to the governor of Pennsylvania. But his council decided that when England had allowed William Penn's "Holy Experiment," it had overturned the law against Catholic services, at least in Pennsylvania.

That was not the end of prejudice against Catholics, and St. Joseph's Church continued to keep a low profile. It doesn't even look like a church on the outside, and even today it might not be noticed from Walnut Street. It has no real front. The Walnut Street entrance is like a side door, and the other entrance is still through the old courtyard off Willings Alley.

St. Mary's was built in 1763 when the congregation of St. Joseph's outgrew the first church. Eighty-five percent of the two parishes are remembered as patriots, many of them either Irish or German.

At St. Joseph's and St. Mary's, the interiors have been changed over the years. St. Mary's also was enlarged, so that only two of its outside walls are original.

At St. Mary's, the carved wood baptismal font with its marble basin dated 1791 is a reminder of the period.

John Adams, who became our second president, attended services at many churches. He was a rather strict Protestant, and he was astonished by the large picture of the Crucifixion behind the altar at St. Mary's. Today, there is a stained-glass window showing the same scene.

Holy Trinity, founded as an offshoot of St. Mary's, was built two years after the Constitutional Convention, specifically to serve the German population. Inside the church, the stations of the cross are still written in German.

The outside of Holy Trinity is a good example of a kind of brickwork called "Flemish bond." The bricks are alternately laid lengthwise and endwise to make a stronger wall.

A Place to Worship

CONSTITUTION QUIZ 7

1. The final draft of the Constitution was written mostly by a one-legged New Yorker who represented Pennsylvania. True or false?

2. Some framers of the Constitution wanted senators and the president to serve without pay. True or false?

3. At one point, the framers of the Constitution considered having three presidents. True or false?

4. The delegates considered only two ways of electing the president, by the people or by Congress. True or false?

5. Benjamin Franklin proposed that judges should be picked by other lawyers. True or false?

6. If no candidate for the presidency receives a majority of the total votes, the president is chosen by:
   a. another election held on the first Tuesday of December.
   b. the Supreme Court, from the qualified candidates.
   c. the House, from among the three candidates who received the most votes.
   d. the Senate, from among the two candidates who received the most votes.

7. Why did the 12th Amendment make presidential electors vote separately for the president and the vice president?

8. Congress is forbidden to suspend *habeas corpus* except in time of rebellion or invasion. What is *habeas corpus?*

9. Congress is forbidden to pass a bill of attainder or an ex post facto law. What are these?

10. Why do all tax bills have to start in the House of Representatives, with the Senate only allowed to suggest amendments?

(Answers: Page 75)

Excerpt from "A Prayer for the Country," recited in English and Hebrew by Jewish congregations on the adoption of the Constitution:

"We beseech thee O Lord to have the United States Senators and Representatives of the United States and all the rulers of the Land under thy Holy Protection . . . that Knowledge, Religion and Piety, Arts and Sciences may increase, and that Agriculture, Manufacture, Trade and Commerce may flow."

CONSTITUTION QUIZ 8

1. Slavery was a delicate point in negotiations at the convention and is mentioned frequently in the Constitution. True or false?

2. It was finally decided by the Convention to count slaves as people, the same as non-slaves.

3. Why does the Constitution forbid members of Congress from holding any other public office?

4. Which of these statements regarding the states is specified in the Constitution?
   a. The states are guaranteed a representative form of government.
   b. The governors of the states must be of the same political party as the president.
   c. The states have the right to make treaties with foreign countries.
   d. The states are allowed to impose their own import taxes.

5. The Constitution of the United States was signed:
   a. by all members of the Constitutional Convention.
   b. by the delegates from the large states only.
   c. by 39 members of the convention.
   d. only by George Washington.

6. Most of the framers ended up rich men. True or false?

7. Which of the following is *not* a service that the judicial branch of the federal government gives to the people?
   a. Settling disputes between states.
   b. Interpreting the Constitution and laws.
   c. Keeping the United States on good terms with other nations.
   d. Keeping federal and state governments within limits of their authority.

(Answers: Page 75)

A PLACE TO WORSHIP

A PLACE TO WORSHIP

WITH RELIGION, THERE'S LOTS TO DO AND THINK ABOUT

1. The delegates to the Constitutional Convention often visited churches other than their own. Attend a service of a religion that you don't know. How is it like what you expected? How is it different?

2. Compare a service with a service of the same religion in 1787. If you lived in 1787, what would your Sabbath be like?

3. "Sunday toys" were toys that could be used to illustrate a Bible story. They could be used for quiet play on the Sabbath, when unnecessary activity was forbidden in most families. They were sometimes playing cards (but not for Quakers or some Protestants), puzzles, dolls or wooden toys. Imagine you are living in 1787, and your mother asks you to take care of your little brother or sister on Sunday afternoon. What can you make, or what toys of your own can you use to tell the stories of:

- Joseph and the coat of many colors?
- Moses and the Ten Commandments?
- Daniel and the lions' den?

4. Old churchyards often have interesting gravestones. Get permission from a church or synagogue to visit one and make a "gravestone rubbing." Rubbings are actually a way of tracing a stone carving onto paper — perhaps an angel's head, or words or dates from the gravestone. You will need a peeled crayon, a piece of white shelf paper or brown wrapping paper, and one other person to help.

One person holds the paper in place while the other pesron rubs the side of the crayon firmly across the paper over the spot to be traced. An impression from the stone should appear as you work.

5. This guide contains descriptions of early religious buildings for Quakers, Episcopalians, Jews, Catholics, Methodists and African Methodist-Episcopalians. How many religious institutions are represented in your neighborhood? Is there a larger variety of sects now than in 1787?

6. Match the following signers of the Constitution with their religious belief or church:

A. George Washington	1. Attended the "Church of the Patriots."
B. Jared Ingersoll	2. A "deist," who believed in a supreme being, but who did not belong to any church.
C. Ben Franklin	3. Not a Philadelphian, but who is buried in Christ Church graveyard.
D. Pierce Butler	4. Was married at Gloria Dei Church.

(Answers: Page 75)

Old Pine Street Church

412 Pine St. 925-8051.

Thirty-five members of Old Pine Street fought as officers under George Washington during the Revolution, and the church, built in 1768, was known afterward as "the church of the patriots." In 1787, its members were probably still recovering from the Revolutionary War. The British had used their church as a hospital and then a stable during the war and had used every bit of available wood, including the window frames, for firewood. It is said that in the days before the Revolution, the old box pews were so tall that a man could stand in them and not be seen.

The British also buried more than 100 Hessian troops in a trench along the east wall, where they remain. The walls are about all that's left of the original church.

We know from church history that by 1796 restoration was complete and pews were rented, a common arrangement in churches of the time. History also tells us that the sexton was stationed at the door with a rod to keep unruly children and dogs out of the church.

The church's great patriot pastor, George Duffield — the British actually put a price on his head — is buried in what is now the basement of the church. Jared Ingersoll, a signer of the Constitution, is buried in the churchyard. John Adams frequently attended Old Pine.

A PLACE TO WORSHIP

A PLACE TO WORSHIP

St. Peter's Church and St. Paul's Church

St. Peter's, Third and Pine Streets. 925-5968.

St. Paul's, near Third and Walnut. 351-1400.

Both of these Episcopal churches were built in 1761, but for different reasons.

The parishioners who built St. Paul's had a disagreement with Christ Church and wanted a separate church. But St. Peter's was really part of the Christ Church parish. It was built because the parish was growing so fast that there wasn't enough room at Christ Church. And it was constructed because Philadelphia was growing so fast that people who had built houses south of Walnut Street lived too far from Christ Church. They didn't want to walk more than half a mile on dirty, unpaved streets to go to church.

Of all the Philadelphia churches from this period, St. Peter's has changed the least inside. The large, high-backed box pews are actually the originals, and you can see that not everybody could sit facing the same way in them. In St. Peter's this might have been an advantage, since the altar is at one end and the original "wine-glass" pulpit at the other. The pulpit still has the sounding board over it. This was a common feature in churches, to make the preacher's voice louder — there were no microphones, of course.

The outside of St. Peter's is considered a fine example of Colonial church architecture. It is a very plain brick building with a gently sloping roof and gracefully arching windows. It doesn't really even look like a church, does it? This same simple design is seen somewhat in St. Paul's, Old First Reformed, St. George's and Old Pine Street churches. At St. Peter's, a steeple was added later.

George and Martha Washington often attended services here and sat in the pew (No. 41) belonging to Samuel Powel.

St. Paul's presents the same simple but graceful appearance as St. Peter's, minus the steeple. St. Paul's today is closed as a church, but it did have a lively past.

First, Christ Church members became unhappy and started St. Paul's. Then, during the Revolution, the rector was loyal to England. That was bad enough, but when he preached a sermon one Sunday that criticized "rebels," that was the last straw. The congregation threw him out and got along without a minister for the rest of the war.

Church records also relate that one of the church sexton's duties was to keep animals out of the graveyard.

Old First Reformed Church

Fourth and Race Streets. 922-9663.

Old First Reformed was founded by German Protestants, fleeing their country to escape religious persecution. At the time the Constitution was drafted, Old First Reformed was in its second home. The building at Fourth and Race Streets is still used today. The building was dedicated in 1774. There is a story that during the Revolution, the pastor lured Hessian (German) soldiers, who were fighting on the British side, into the church. His preaching was so fiery that it led many of them to desert.

In the church lobby, visitors today can still see the old stone well used to supply water for the church. Under the church are the old crypts where bodies were stored in their coffins during the winter when the ground outside was too cold to dig a grave.

Up in the gallery near the organ is a wooden eagle carved at the time of the Revolution to replace an older decoration, probably a crown. The building was abandoned as a church for a time and used as a paint warehouse. Its interior was ripped out, and it was not completely restored until 1967.

PATHWAY TO THE CONSTITUTION

C. This is the majority vote, but a lot of delegates were very nervous about giving so much power to one person. Eventually, as the convention progressed, the system of "checks and balances" between Congress, the president and the Supreme Court developed to calm those fears.

4. June 4, 1787: The Constitutional Convention is debating whether the executive should have the power to veto laws.

a. You agree with Ben Franklin that it is wrong to give one person so much power.

b. You favor letting the judges (Supreme Court) and the executive *together* veto Congress' bills.

c. You agree with James Madison: The executive will have veto powers, but Congress can vote to override vetoes.

d. You favor a plan to allow the president to have absolute veto over laws he does not like.

(What did the Constitution Framers decide? Go to Page 57.)

A PLACE TO WORSHIP

A PLACE TO WORSHIP

St. George's Church

235 N. Fourth St. 925-7788.

St. George's Church started out when some discontented members of Old First Reformed decided to build a new church. A merchant, a pumpmaker, a candle maker, a shoemaker, a flour dealer, a tailor, a brick layer and a mason — and their wives — worked to get the walls up. But then they ran out of money, and the men were soon in debtors' prison. The building was put to auction to get them out, and the Methodist community of the time bought it and finished it in 1769.

St. George's is a good place to compare the glass windows of the early days with modern windows. In the old glass in the north windows, you see ripples. The modern glass in the south wall is smooth and clear. Plain glass doesn't seem like a luxury to us, but it was in 1787. Many people couldn't afford glass windows in their homes, but paid to put them in their churches and meeting houses.

John Adams, who was a Congregationalist when at home in Boston, visited St. George's in Philadelphia. He found that the preacher (Capt. Thomas Webb, who wore a sword and a green eye patch) could fire the imagination and that the singing of the hymns was "very sweet and soft indeed."

In the church itself are the original long-handled collection baskets from the 1700s, and a foot-warmer, a metal box that was filled with hot bricks or coals and brought into the pew in winter. The church museum holds a Bible and a watch that belonged to the great Methodist traveling preacher Francis Asbury, and a silver chalice sent to Asbury by John Wesley, the English founder of Methodism.

St. George's is the oldest Methodist church in continuous use in the world. In the 1920s, there was a plan to tear down the church to make room for what is now the Benjamin Franklin Bridge. After a national protest, the path of the bridge was changed, and St. George's became known as "the church that moved the bridge."

Mikveh Israel

44 N. Fourth St., between Market and Arch Streets. 922-5446.

Congregation Mikveh Israel, the second-oldest Jewish congregation in the United States, was spiritual home to Haym Solomon. He was one of the two men (Robert Morris was the other) who gave the most money to pay for the Revolution. The synagogue was also home to Nathan Levy, whose ship brought the Liberty Bell to the city.

The first Philadelphia synagogue, built in 1782, survived early financial difficulties in the year after the Constitutional Convention, when its members appealed to fellow citizens for help. Benjamin Franklin's name and pledge of five pounds can be seen at the top of the subscription list.

Today the congregation's cemetery, on Spruce Street between Eighth and Ninth Streets, remains.

A new synagogue was built on Fourth Street in 1976, and its Sephardic services are exactly as they would have been in 1787.

John Adams, on a visit to St. Mary's Catholic Church in 1774:

"This afternoon, led by curiosity and good company, I strolled away to mother church, or rather to grandmother church. I mean the Romish Chapel. I heard a good, short essay upon the duty of parents to their children, founded in justice and charity, to take care of their interests, temporal and spiritual. The music, consisting of an organ and a choir of singers, went all the afternoon except sermon time. And the assembly chanted most sweetly and exquisitely."

Mother Bethel

419 S. Sixth St. (Richard Allen Avenue) 925-0616.

In 1787, a notable young man in the Methodist church was the black preacher Richard Allen. He was licensed to preach in 1784 while still a slave, and he bought his freedom for $2,000 in 1786, when he was 22.

There are many stories about why Allen and another former slave, Absalom Jones, left St. George's Church in 1787. Some say the white congregation objected to blacks kneeling at the altar rail; some say blacks were made to sit in a special part of the church. Others say, though, that St. George's treated blacks and whites equally.

For whatever reason, Allen and Jones did leave St. George's and founded the Free Africa Society. The society's first place of worship was an old blacksmith shop that was hauled to the piece of land that Allen had bought on Sixth Street, where Mother Bethel stands today.

After a few years, Jones' followers chose to unite with the Episcopal Church. Allen's remained separate, and the church took on the name "African Methodist Episcopal Church." It celebrates its 200th birthday along with the Constitution.

Allen and Jones were respected citizens as well as religious leaders. At the time the Constitution was being written, they were already campaigning against slavery. Mother Bethel served as a station on the "Underground Railroad" before and during the Civil War.

The present building was finished in 1794. In its museum can be seen the wooden pulpit and benches Allen himself carved for his first church. Allen's tomb is also at the church.

LIFESTYLE 1787

Summer away from home was no picnic

How did the delegates fare away from home for four months in the summer of '87? It wasn't always easy, although some of them did bring their families along.

George Washington came alone. He and Martha would later live in Philadelphia as president and first lady. But this summer he accepted the kind offer of a room at the home of Pennsylvania delegate Robert Morris, just a block from Independence Hall.

Washington was quiet and undemanding. He would often slip into the house and go to his room without speaking to anyone.

Other delegates rented rooms at boarding houses or in the city's inns, such as the Indian Queen on Fourth Street, or City Tavern. There, they could sit late over supper, talk till all hours and toddle off to bed without leaving the inn.

One delegate staying at City Tavern, Dr. William Samuel Johnson of Connecticut, noted the weather every day in his diary. He didn't have much good to say about it.

The Southern delegates probably got along better in the heat and humidity. They were used to it and had brought along lighter clothes. For New Englanders, with their woolen clothes, it must have been torture.

One of the South Carolina Pinckneys brought the members of his family along, but left them in New York because he thought Philadelphia was an unhealthy place in summer. This proved all too true a few years later, when the great yellow fever epidemic killed thousands.

Yellow fever was spread by mosquito bite, though no one knew it at the time. And there were mosquitoes aplenty in Philadelphia in summer, with no window screens to keep them out.

As Independence Day approached, the convention was deadlocked in the fight between the big and the small states for their share of Congress. The delegates took the Fourth of July off and went around town trying to look cheerful.

There was a parade, there were church services, and people gathered at City Tavern and the Indian Queen to celebrate independence and toast to the future. Then it was back to business.

The heat broke around mid-July for a little while, and everyone got a little sleep for a change.

Being in Philadelphia wasn't all bad. After all, there were flies everywhere else, too. And it was the center of the New World.

Delegates could enjoy good company, fine dining, and interesting plays and concerts, plus the latest books and newspapers from America and abroad.

They could — and did — take excursions to the farm country to the west, or travel along the Delaware, or visit world-famous botanist John Bartram and his gardens on the Schuylkill. There they could take the ferry right across to Gray's Inn for a visit and refreshments with the Gray family.

Most of all, they probably enjoyed visiting people at home in Philadelphia. There is no doubt that the best homes of Philadelphia were open to them. Ben Franklin often entertained one or more delegates in his cool, pleasant garden so near Independence Hall. Some played musical instruments, and they might get together for a little jam session, 1700s style.

Still, if the heat hadn't broken for a little while in July, they might have all just gone home in a temper. In August the heat was back. Johnson recorded only two cool days in three weeks.

The heat was on again in September, physically and mentally. Behind closed doors, Ben Franklin begged for a united front. They signed. They went public. On Sept. 19, the Pennsylvania Packet, a pro-Constitution newspaper, gave its entire space over to the new document. "We, the People . . ."

The people, many of them, were shocked. They argued in newspapers and rioted in the streets. But in less than a year, the work of the delegates had been ratified by 11 states. The Constitution was the law of the land. Four months of working and living in the hot, noisy, special city of Philadelphia had paid off.

PATHWAY TO THE CONSTITUTION

C. The Bill of Rights was added in 1791, after the Constitution had been ratified (1789). Several delegates refused to sign the Constitution largely because no Bill of Rights was included.

You've done a good job making up this Constitution. Now you've got to go home and work twice as hard to convince people that they should ratify adopt it.

William Penn's Letters and Inkwell

© Helen I. Driggs, 1987

Answers, "Things to Think About,"

1. Among the best-known privileges it gives us are freedom of religion, freedom of speech, a free press and freedom to assemble and bear arms, and the right to a trial by a jury of our peers, or equals. It also gives us the right to privacy. The Bill of Rights provides for personal freedoms, and many of the delegates believed that the document that formed a government should not get involved with personal fixmatters.

2. Blacks and women. The original Constitution had nothing in it to discourage slavery, and it was not abolished until 1865, when the 13th Amendment was adopted. The 15th Amendment gave black males the right to vote. Women were not guaranteed the right to vote until the 19th Amendment was ratified in 1920.

3. After Virginia seceded from the union at the start of the Civil War in 1861, West Virginia broke off from Virginia. It was admitted to the union as a separate state two years later. It remained a separate state after the war. That was possible, although Virginia did not approve the action, because Virginia was at war with the United States and not considered a part of the country at the time.

4. Among other things, the United States would be back in the position of the original 13 states, having to beg, more or less, for funds for highways, the running of the government, public service programs for health and education, and national defense. It is interesting to note that a major source of tax income, the federal income tax, wasn't adopted until 1913, when ratification of the 16th Amendment was declared.

5. Military service has always been controversial. As early as the Revolutionary War, Americans disagreed about it. What's your opinion?

Answer to cryptogram,

We the People of the United States, in Order to form a more perfect Union, establish Justice, insure domestic Tranquility, provide for the common defence, promote the general welfare, and secure the Blessings of Liberty to ourselves and our Posterity, do ordain and establish this Constitution for the United States of America.

Answers to Question 6,

A-2, C-2. Both Washington and Franklin believed simply in the existence of a supreme being, so they have been called "deists."

B-1. Jared Ingersoll attended and is buried at Old Pine, "Church of the Patriots."

D-3. Pierce Butler was a delegate from South Carolina. He is buried in Philadelphia at Christ Church.

None of the delegates was married at Gloria Dei. Betsy Ross, the woman who is said to have designed the first American flag, was married there. She might have loved to be a delegate, but no woman attended the convention, or even voted, in those days.

Answers, Constitution Quiz 1

1. True. All the meetings of the convention were held in secret. Today, neither the public nor the press would tolerate that.
2. d
3. a
4. True. Charles Pinckney of South Carolina believed that all public officials should have enough property to be "independent and respectable." Franklin said that this insulted the common people and that some of the biggest rogues he had ever known were the richest rogues.

Answers, Quiz 2

1. In early January, when the president of the Senate opens the sealed ballots of the electors from each state in the presence of the Congress.
2. False. Ben Franklin had recommended that the convention hire a chaplain, but the convention didn't have the money.
3. c
4. True. In 1783, a band of Pennsylvania soldiers surrounded Congress when it was in session, demanding back pay. Congress begged the Philadelphia police to rescue them, but the police refused. This is why the framers wanted a separate national capital with its own police force.
5. More than 8,000. The original ratio was one representative for every 30,000 people. In 1929, Congress voted to limit the number of representatives to 435.

Answers, Quiz 3

1. False. Most of the delegates paid for all their own expenses.
2. c
3. b

Answers, Quiz 4

1. d
2. No. The Constitution says that each state shall have at least one representative.
3. False. New Hampshire arrived late, New York left early and Rhode Island didn't show up at all.
4. True. The reason for keeping the sessions secret was to silence wild rumors like this one and others. For instance, there was one that said Rhode Island would be expelled from the union and another that said all the states would be combined into three new super-states.
5. Men such as James Wilson and Ben Franklin realized that there was a lot of anti-Constitution sentiment in western Pennsylvania. They wanted to push ratification as fast as possible before the anti-Constitution forces could be organized.

When the legislature met in Philadelphia to authorize a ratification convention, the anti-Constitution members boycotted the meeting so that there wouldn't be a quorum and business couldn't be conducted. However, a pro-Constitution street mob of artisans and merchants found the anti-Constitution delegates hiding out.

The mob broke down the door, seized and beat several of the hiding delegates and dragged them, battered and bruised in torn clothing, through the streets to the meeting hall, where they forced them into seats.

Another reason Franklin wanted Pennsylvania to ratify quickly is that he wanted the new federal capital to be located in the state. He hoped that quick ratification would improve Pennsylvania's chances.

Answers, Quiz 5

1. False. Three states — Connecticut, Massachusetts and Georgia — did not ratify the Bill of Rights until 1941, more than 150 years late.
2. a
3. It is generally considered to mean a citizen born in America.

Answers, Quiz 6

1. False. The Northern delegates wanted slaves regarded as property. In that way, the federal government could tax their owners for their slaves' value, but they would not be counted as people entitled to congressional representation. Southerners took the reverse view. They didn't want to be taxed on the value of their slaves as property, and they wanted them counted as the basis of congressional representation.
2. Voting rights. Voting rights is the subject of six of the 26 amendments. (The 15th Amendment gave black males the right to vote; the 17th gave people the right to elect U.S. senators directly; the 19th gave women the right to vote; the 23d gave citizens of the District of Columbia the right to vote; the 24th banned a tax on voting, and the 26th lowered the voting age to 18.)
3. No. Only about 5 percent of the population had the right to vote. In many states, voting was limited to white, male, Christian, adult property owners.
4. False. Many delegates were afraid that a rich government such as England's might send a lot of secret agents to America to quickly become citizens, get elected to public office and secretly seize control of the government from within.

Answers, Quiz 7

1. True. Gouverneur Morris, who had one wooden leg and a withered arm, wrote most of the final draft. He was a New Yorker living in Philadelphia.
2. True. Charles Cotesworth Pinckney of South Carolina and Ben Franklin of Pennsylvania thought senators and the president should be wealthy men serving only for the honor of it.
3. True. Edmund Randolph of Virginia proposed three presidents for three major regions of the 13 states — New England, the Middle Atlantic and the South. He thought that having one president was too much like having a king.
4. False. The delegates debated six methods of electing the president: First, by the people directly; second, by the Congress; third, by the state governors; fourth, by electors elected by the people; fifth, by the people voting for their three favorites, and finally, by lottery.
5. True. It is the Scottish method, he said. Lawyers would always pick the most competent lawyers to be judges, so as to eliminate competition for clients.
6. c
7. Originally, whoever got the most votes was president, and the runner-up was vice president. That sometimes resulted in a president from one political party and a vice president from another.
8. Literally, *habeas corpus* is Latin for "produce the body." If you are arrested, you must be brought into open court promptly and either charged with a crime or freed.
9. A bill of attainder is a law that convicts a person of a crime without an open trial.An ex post facto law is one that makes something done in the past a crime even if it was legal at the time.
10. The Founding Fathers felt that the people would be the ones who had to pay the taxes and that the house of Congress elected directly by them should decide what those taxes should be. At first, only the House was directed elected by the public. (Until the 17th Amendment, providing for popular election of U.S. senators, was ratified in 1913, senators were chosen by the state legislatures.)

Answers, Quiz 8

1. True and false. It was a delicate point, but the word "slave" is never mentioned in the Constitution, even though the document has provisions for extraditing fugitive slaves, regulating the slave trade, and counting slaves as three-fifths of a person apiece for representation.
2. False. Slaves counted as three-fifths of a person apiece for representation purposes.
3. The framers feared they would create profitable government jobs and appoint themselves.
4. a
5. c
6. False. Ten of the 39 signers of the Constitution ended up bankrupt or on the verge of financial ruin.
7. c

Hint to finding the signers of the Constitution: There are no extra A's in the puzzle. Every A that appears is used in at least one name.

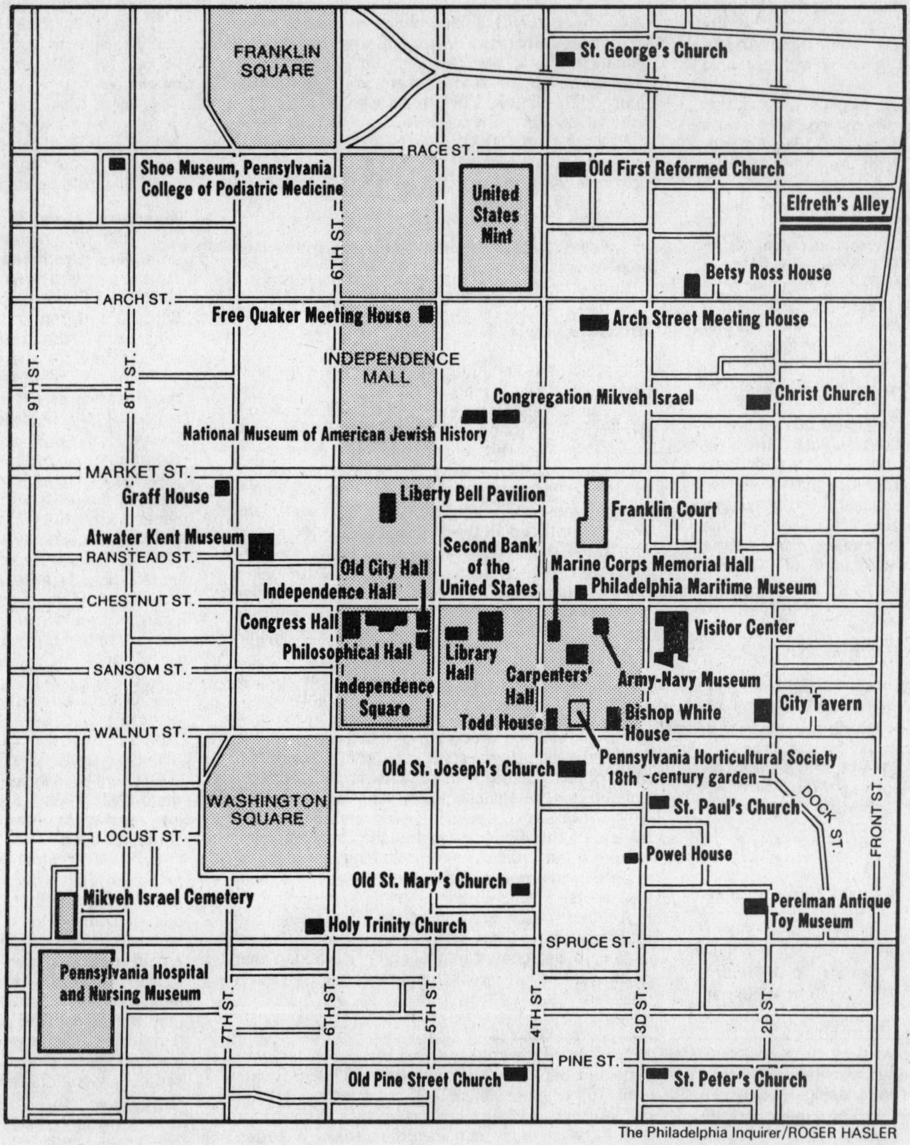

The Philadelphia Inquirer/ROGER HASLER

NOTES

NOTES

NOTES

NOTES